Memories
of an **Old Geezer**

Lonie B. Adcock

MEMORIES of an Old Geezer
Lonie B. Adcock

copyright © 2011 Lonie B. Adcock
all rights reserved

ISBN 978-0-9833643-4-4

cover and interior design, Dekie Hicks

www.wheredeponypress.com
Rome Georgia

printed in the U.S.A.

To my wife, Eunice W. Adcock, who stood by me faithfully with her red pen in hand. She did as much work on this book as I did.

To my family and friends who encouraged my writing and urged me to put it in book form.

To Dekie Hicks who made it possible by pulling it all together.

Contents

Introduction — vi

Part 1 Early Childhood

Face in the Window	1
Life in Euharlee	4
A Big Black Car and an Outside Bath	7
Keg Whiskey	10
Shiny Shoes	12
Lullaby	14
Gypsy	17
Hermit	20
Halloween	22
Sack Fishing	25
Kick the Can	28
Skinny Dipping	31
First Hug	34
Bully	37
Glue Britches	41
Wee Wee	44
Play Ball	48
Toothbrush	51
Bush Arbor	54
Ride It Cowboy	58
White Flower	61
Broken Gun	63
House on the Hill	67
Barber Shop	71
Last Dance	73
Jingle Money	76
Valentine	80

Part 2 Teen Years

Rabbit Hunting with a Rock	83
Ghost	86
Ghost Hill	87
Drink the Punch	93

Part 3 Army Days

Lady Libery	97
Christmas Away From Home	104
Roller Skating	107
Peter	112

Part 4 Police Work

Christmas in the City	119
Cisco	121
Squeaky	123
Opossum	126
Old Timers' Bench	129
Fine China	135
The Return of the Bully	138
Donkey Kong	140
Joy Riding	144
American Hero	147
Fore!	150
Railroad Ghost	153
Monkey Business	157
Walk the Walk	160
Last Laugh	164
Run Shorty, Run!	167

Hang On, Cowboy	171	Don't Forget Me, Mister	220
Pants Up, Pants Down	174	Ghost Doll	224
The Nude Burglar	176		
Snake in the Purse	179	**Part 5 This and That**	
Crap Game	182		
Angel	186	1911	230
Albuquerque	189	Franklin Auto	232
Blue Angel	192	USA	234
Streakers	196	Born on the Fourth of July	237
UFO	199	Star Spangled Banner	239
Mud Bath	202	Flag Draped Coffin	241
Cemetery Lights	207	Looking Back	243
Gamma Rays	211	Butts	247
Light in the Window	214	Do You Know?	249
Miracle	217	A Little Bit of Humor	250

Introduction

I was born Lonie Burton Adcock in Kingston, Bartow County, Georgia on July 4, 1930. My father was Landum Benjamin Adcock and my mother was Margaret Melissia Haney Adcock. I was one of six children, three boys and three girls. The girls came first—Zonie, Lillie and Gracy—followed by the boys, Lonie, Julian and Wesley. My father had two sons by a previous marriage, Will and John. Weldon, who I frequently mention, was the son of Will.

Lonie's father (center) with Will (left) and John (right)

Landum Benjamin Adcock was an evangelist preacher for the Church of Christ. Margaret Haney Adcock was a housewife. As his family grew, my father became a farmer. He farmed for a few years then moved to Rome and worked at construction. The youngest girl, Gracy, died at a young age. My father died in 1941. Upon my father's death, my Mother worked as a seamstress.

I attended Elm Street Elementary, Neely School and Old Boys' High on the hill. By the time I hit high school, my sisters had married and moved out on their own. Mother became disabled and couldn't work. I was the oldest boy, so the burden of making a living was on my back. I was fourteen and, unlike other boys, I enjoyed going to school. I knew that there was no other solution to my family's lack of income, so I quit and went to work. My first job was that of a short order cook. Then I went into construction work at age fifteen.

In 1951 I was inducted into the Armed Forces of the United States of America. During the processing period I went to the library on the post and found manuals on the Signal Corp and read them. When we were tested to see what branch of service we were suited for, I was placed in the Army Signal Corp. I trained in Signal construction and was sent to Germany as part of the occupation troops. Shortly after we arrived peace was signed and we became NATO Forces. We went to work replacing telephones lines and other types of communication equipment. I was discharged in 1952 and came home.

On November 7, 1953, I married Eunice Lois Worley whom I have known since she was five and I was ten. Eunice and I still reside in Rome, Georgia. I worked for a while in upholstery then drifted into mechanic work. I was still looking for a job that I wanted to make into a career. I found that career on the Rome police force. I joined the Rome Police Department in 1958 and retired from there in 1990. I worked with and met a lot of good people in my time with the department. I both walked the street as a patrol officer and rode in patrol cars. I was promoted to the rank of Detective Sergeant, went back in uniform as a Sergeant and was later promoted to Lieutenant. I was a shift supervisor until retirement.

Even though I had to quit school at fourteen, I never quit reading and learning. That's why I count reading and writing as my hobbies today. And fishing, too! Not necessarily in that order.

In the following pages, I will mention many old and dear friends. I mention Houston Duggan Farmer, who is still alive today and with whom I remain great friends. Also, Dora Mae and Baby Alma who I still count among my friends. Jimmy Chapman, Robert Roberts, and Eddie Cantrell have all passed away now. Duke Hughes was my best buddy right before I went into the army. He passed away in a car accident years ago.

Part 1

EARLY CHILDHOOD

Face in the Window

When I was a small boy living in White, in Bartow County, we lived in an old plantation house that had been used as a hospital when Sherman went though on his way to Atlanta. Highway 411 ran in front of this house and a railroad ran parallel with 411. Highway 140 ran on the right side of our house. A small building sat near our house and next to that building was a one-room jail. The house was a large one that had, as best I can recall, about fourteen rooms and a wrap-around porch.

I had two half brothers who were a lot older than I was. One of them was married and had started a family of his own. He lived in one side of the house. There was plenty of room and then some to spare. At the time I was the baby with three older sisters. My three sisters and I were my father's third family. In the end there were six of us—three girls and three boys. My father and my half brother were farming and making willow furniture on the side.

My father and my half brother had an old truck. They would make a load of willow furniture and take it to the big city of Atlanta to sell. What they didn't sell they would bring back home and display on the big porch. People would stop and buy it. My mother was always there to greet the people who wanted to stop and look. I remember when a man and woman stopped and before they left, the man told my mother that her father standing in the window had a beautiful headdress. We didn't understand what he meant. After he left we children went on playing in the yard and my mother went back in to the house.

Soon after, one night we were all at the table eating supper when a big noise that sounded like someone tearing down the back door startled us. My father got up and went to investigate. Soon he was back, shaking his head. My mother asked what had happened.

"Nothing," he said. "The door is okay."

There was another time when we were all in the living room and heard what sounded like a dog running though the house. We all went to look for the dog and found him out in the front yard away from the house. The dog had to be fed out in the yard for he wouldn't come in the house. All the time that we lived there, the dog never came into the house. Small boy that I was, I tried to pick him up and carry him into the house but he would scramble away from me on the porch.

Lonie with his sister Lillie Mae

One day my mother and father had gone down to White to get groceries. The girls were playing under a big tree that sat away from the house. I had an old car tire that I was rolling toward the house and back to the tree where the girls were. I started toward the house and the girls suddenly hollered for me to come back. Not knowing what was happening, I turned the tire loose and ran back to my sisters. They were pointing toward an upstairs window. I looked up and remember seeing what looked like a man with a headdress of some sort on his head. The tire rolled down to the porch and stopped in an upright position without anything holding it. My sisters ran over, grabbed me and started running to the big tree which was a safe distance away. We sat under that tree and didn't go back to the house until our parents got home! Even with our parents there, we hesitated going into the house.

It was just a few days later that we moved from there. As we grew up my sisters and I would talk about the figure in the window. Our parents would laugh at us but we knew what we had seen. The apparition looked like a Native American in full dress. I remember that the headdress didn't look like the kind that they wore in the movies. It looked more like a wrap-around turban with a lot of beautiful feathers in it.

Life in Euharlee

I recently opened up the *Rome News Tribune* and to my surprise there was a picture of the old Hardin Bridge. I didn't have to read the article to know where the bridge was. I spent my young childhood close by it. As you crossed the bridge coming from Kingston or Euharlee there was a house that sat in a field on the right side of the road. At that time, there was on the left side of the road a small building that some said used to be a house. I remember that back then it was about to fall in. No one lived in it. All the land on both sides of the road was owned by a family named Dodd.

John, a half brother who was in the Army, used to come and see us quite often. In the summer, the river would get low revealing a row of rocks that you could walk across. Across the river there was an opening in the bank. One day John walked across and looked in the opening. He came back and reported that it was a cave. He wouldn't go in it until he had someone with him. My parents weren't going to let me go with him.

Later, he brought back a couple of his Army buddies and they went with him into the cave. They stayed over there for several hours before they came back. They had something in sacks. I never got to see what it was for they put it in the trunk of the car. John stated that the cave was as big as a room. What was there I never found out because we moved before I got big enough to walk across the rocks.

My father was known among the people as the Herb Doctor. He had a herb for just about any ailment, everything from sassafras tea to calumets root. There was a remedy for the cough that would make you well if it didn't kill you. I am sure that some of you have heard of yellow root and mullein. Those were two sure cures for anything. I can't knock it for I came though the years with flying colors. Must have been some good in those herbs.

In the spring, my father would get his bag, take a cloth sack made for that purpose and go get his herbs. In the fall it was the same thing over again. I remember he took me and my three sisters with him on a trip into the woods looking for herbs. He also carried us over to what is known as the Salt Peter Caves. There are several openings as you go down into the caves, one of which is as big as a two-storey house. It's a sight to see or it was back then. I took my wife and some friends to the caves some forty odds years ago. It has been so long since I was there I doubt if I could find them now. Back when I took my wife, the road to the caves was just about gone.

I can still remember the old Hardin Bridge. I know that it's been seventy years or more since we lived there. It had an iron structure but had a wooden floor. The planks ran crossways and on top of them were several boards running lengthwise from one end of the bridge to the other. There were two rows of these boards that you kept your wheels on as you crossed the bridge. If other people were on the bridge, you had to wait until they got across. There was no passing on the boards that you ran on. I don't believe that the old bridge was wide enough for two vehicles side by side. Can you imagine that about the time you got to the bridge here came a man on a wagon pulled by horses? It happened back in those days.

John would take me and Weldon riding on the weekend when he come home. We went to Euharlee quite a lot. He would take us to a store that sat on the right as you went into town. As I remember there was a blacksmith shop across the street from the general store. I seem to recall several buildings being there. John would get Weldon and me a cold drink and tell us to watch the car while he went back inside. You can bet no one bothered the car for we sat there by it and drank the cold soda pop. John would bring back a small paper sack and put it in a pocket on the door. We never knew what he had in the bag. I remember that after we got back home and ate supper he would go out to the car and stay a while. I remember smelling a funny odor on his breath.

I also remember a big spring of water on the left side of the road before you got to the bridge. A homemade bench was there where you could sit down and have a cool drink of water. Dippers made from gourds hung from the limb of a tree. No one thought anything of getting a gourd dipper, rinsing it out and having a dipper of water. Now you would never drink from a gourd dipper hanging from a tree limb open to the public. There aren't too many springs that you can drink from. There were so many cool springs of water back in those days and everyone took care of them. A cool spring of water on your place was like having money in the bank.

The last time I was in that area was when I carried my wife and some friends to see Salt Peter Caves. We went over the old bridge and down to where the house in which I spent most of my early years sat in a field. The frame of the old house was still standing. I remember having some great times there. We went on down the road and as I remember the little church was still standing. That trip was close to fifty years ago. I have been thinking about going back to see what the last fifty years have changed. I know that the old bridge is gone, but it is still alive and well in my memory. I can close my eyes and see a small barefooted boy running the wooden board on the bridge in front of his father.

A Big Black Car and an Outside Bath

John, my half brother who was in the Army in Atlanta, would sometimes come home on the weekend. I remember John was in the Cavalry and would tell me stories about riding the horses. He also drove the biggest black car that I can ever remember seeing. I believe it was a Franklin. I remember thinking that it was the prettiest thing that I'd ever seen. I made up my mind that some day I would own a big black automobile.

My other half brother who lived down the road from us had a boy about my age named Weldon. He was my best friend then and remained so though the years. John would put me in the car and we would go get Weldon and ride to the big city of Kingston. In those days Kingston was a busy place. John would park on the main street in front of a store that sold dry goods. John would leave Weldon and me in the car and go up the street to what was called an opera house. He would stay a while and then come back and back home we would go. It was the thrill of a lifetime to sit up in that black car and watch the people stare as we went by. John would blow the horn and that would set Weldon and me to laughing.

There was a big spring in our yard where we got our water. Milk and butter were kept cold in that and it flowed into a stream down to the river. It was a stream that ran year long, never going dry. One time John came home for a few days and started a project. He carried rocks from the fields around the house and piled them up at the foot of the stream close to the river. I would carry a small one and throw it on the pile. He drove into Kingston and bought a bag of concrete mix. Then he dug both a hole and a trench and placed a pipe in a trench and ran it from the hole. He lined the bottom of the hole with the rocks collected from the field. That rock floor looked like something you would only see uptown! When he finished, he stood back and looked at it.

He shook his head and, picking up the fishing poles, said, "Come on Burt. Let's go catch our supper."

I remember that he stayed around for a few days then went back to camp. He was stationed in Atlanta. He came back the next weekend, driving up in the big, black, shiny automobile. After a while he put on work clothes and went to look at his outside bath, as he called it. He knelt down and inspected each rock that he had laid in the floor. He had made a set of steps leading down into the bath. He picked up his shovel and began to dig a trench from the stream to his outside bathroom. With the ditch cut the way he wanted it, he took the remaining rock and laid them on the bottom of it. He had the rock in such a position that when the water built up, it poured over into the bath like a waterfall. If any piece of trash fell in the stream, you could pick it up before it went over the waterfall.

I sat with him and watched as the pool filled with water. It would fill up so far and then the overflow would go though the pipe and pour back in the stream. I remember looking at the water as it poured though the pipe and wondered how you could take a bath in that small amount of water. John moved down the steps with a rock and placed it on top of the pipe. He had the rock attached to a rope which was on the end of a stick. I still couldn't see how you could take a bath in there.

The pool began to fill and I watched as the water rose to the top. He pulled the stick with the rope on it and the rock moved. The water rushed though the pipe and left the pool with about six inches of water in the bottom. The John went to the house and I followed him. He got a bar of soap from my mother and went into the back bed room. Soon he came back out wearing swim trunks.

I watched as he cleaned all of the rock with soap. He let the pool fill up; then he emptied it. When he had the rock and the concrete joint clean, he soaped up and sat down in the pool. The water came up under his arms. I could see how you could take a bath in there now. He soaped up, rinsed off, then released the water. He

EARLY CHILDHOOD

put the rock back in place and sat in the cool water, smiling.

"Hey Burt," he said, "go put you on something and come in. it's nice and cool!"

I ran to the house and told my other what John wanted me to do. With a short pair of cutoff pants, I went back to join him. I never will forget sitting in that cool water on that hot day with my half brother. I remember that he talked to me as if I were a grown up.

I spent many a day sitting in the pool that John had made. When he would come home and after we had done some fishing, we would sit in the pool of cool water for a long time.

Then John quit coming to see us and I couldn't understand it. My father told me that John was in a foreign country and couldn't come home at that time. It was hard for a small child who was fond of his brother to understand why he quit coming to see him.

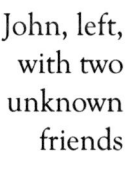

John, left, with two unknown friends

Keg Whiskey

One spring, we had a lot of rain and the river rose out of its banks. My parents were afraid that if the water got up too high we would have to move. A watchful eye was kept on the river. One morning the water was up almost to the house when we got up. A curve in the river made a ditch that ran back into the bank behind the house. Trees covered the mouth of the ditch which was full of water.

John had been outside doing something when he came in and got my father. "I want to show you something," he said.

I went outside with them to see what was happening. There in the ditch was a bunch of small barrels that had floated up next to the bank. I remember watching as John took a stick and pulled one of the barrels up to where he could lift it onto dry land. He and my father began to look it over. John went to get a hammer and began to tap on the barrel. A peg in the top came loose. He smelled the peg and motioned for my father to do the same. John got a long stick and began to pull all the barrels to the bank. There must have been eight or ten of them. I have no idea where they came from. I know now what was in the barrel was whiskey, but I had no idea at the time.

The barrels sat in the yard all day and no one came to check on them. I remember that night standing on the back porch watching John put some of the barrels in the trunk of his big black car. I know he took them with him when he left early the next day. He said his leave was up and he had to get back to camp. I just bet he had himself quite a party before he went back to camp! Some fellows came down later in the day and picked up what was left of the barrels. I never knew who the fellows were who picked up the remaining barrels. I heard the grown ups talking about a place on the river close to Euharlee that made some of the best moonshine you had ever tasted.

Shiny Shoes

I remember a time when my father woke me up to ask if I wanted to go to Kingston and get me a new pair of shoes. I jumped out of bed and got ready to go. A new pair of shoes! I couldn't ever remember having a new pair of shoes. I did have shoes to wear in the winter, but they were never new. In later years I kidded my sisters that I had to wear their old shoes when they outgrew them.

My father and I rode into Kingston on Lullaby's truck. It was fall and most of the work around the farm was done, so there was time for the owners of the farm to take everyone to town for supplies. Now back in those days Kingston was a booming town. On a busy Saturday folks would have to park down the road from town and walk in. The street would be full of vehicles and people. We didn't mind a walk because coming to the big city was a thrill! To a country boy who didn't get to town very often, Kingston was a big city.

Daddy wasted no time. When we got to town, he carried me straight to the store where the shoes and clothes were on display. I sat down in a chair and was brought a cloth to wipe off my feet before putting on a pair of socks. A salesman brought out several boxes and set them down for my father to look at. I remember stretching my neck to see what was in the boxes. After looking at all the shoes in the boxes, my feet were measured and a pair of shoes put in front of me. They were high top and black, what people called brogans. They were the prettiest pair of shoes that I had ever seen. I put them on and the salesman tied them for me.

"Stand up," he said. He felt all around the shoes. I walked around in them and my father was satisfied that they were a fit and paid the man. I remember leaving the store as fast as I could. I was afraid the man would take them back.

Once outside I hunted up Weldon who had come with us. My father and Will, my half brother, told Weldon and me to go see the town. See the town I did, for I wanted everyone in town to see my new shiny shoes. Later we sat down at the depot and I stuck my feet out so anyone close by could see my new shoes. It wasn't long before Weldon and I got hungry so we went in search of our fathers.

We searched every store but they were nowhere to be found. I remember Weldon asking, "Do you think they went home without us?"

We decided to head back to the truck and found Lullaby singing and playing guitar with a group of people. He told us that our fathers were still downtown, so we went back and checked again. On the corner where the street turned toward where the road is today was a building that people referred to as the opera house. We crossed the street looked in though the door. There were people sitting at tables drinking something in glasses. We started though the door when a voice said, "Hold on there, young fellows. You can't go in there."

I turned and looked up at the biggest fellow that I had ever seen. "Sir, we're hunting our fathers."

"I'll hunt for you. Stand there and don't move."

We waited until he came back shaking his head. "Not here," he said. "You'll have to look somewhere else."

Being small boys it never occurred to us that the man didn't know who our fathers were. I know now that he didn't want us standing there in the door. There were people coming and going. They all seemed to have enjoyed whatever was inside. Weldon and I went back over to the depot and sat down. It wasn't long before our fathers came and took us to get something to eat.

It had been a long day. I sat on the back of the truck and could hardly wait to show my mother and my sisters my new shiny shoes. I don't know whether anyone today remembers the Endicott Johnson Brogans. After they were worn for a while they would begin to make a squeaking noise when you walked. You had to keep the leather oiled. But to me, it didn't matter if they squeaked. They were shiny and they were new!

Lullaby

One person I remember was a young man named Lullaby. I don't know if he was a member of the Dodd family or a person who worked for them. He drove the big truck that hauled the cotton to the gin. If something was needed from town, he was the one who drove the truck to get it. One thing I do remember is that he had a beat up old guitar that he could make beautiful music on. If he wasn't picking and singing with his guitar, he was singing without it. You would know when he was headed your way because you could hear him singing.

The Dodd family would let Lullaby take the truck on the weekend and carry people who worked on the farm to Kingston. His old beat up guitar was always behind the seat of the truck. The old truck would sound like a train coming down the road when he picked up the people on a Saturday morning. We were his last stop. Then we went across the old wooden bridge and into the big city of Kingston. Lullaby would park the truck in the area where the park is today. Everyone would head for the stores to do some window wishing. After a while the kids would get tired and go back to the truck. It was as if Lullaby was watching for us, for when we got there, he would get his old beat up guitar and sit down against a tree. We would all gather around and he would pick and sing. One song that I remember that he sang was *Froggy Went a Courting*.

The people had a babysitter when Lullaby was around. It wasn't only the kids who would gather around. In just a few minutes he would have a crowd of grown-ups. They would gather around and pretty soon everyone would join in singing with him. He was a lovable character and people enjoyed him. I recall one Saturday morning when we had gotten tired and had gathered around listening to him. There was an unusually large crowd of people that day. They would join in and sing with him on some religious songs. He would play a tune on the guitar and the people would applaud and cheer him.

Suddenly a voice boomed out, "What's going on here? Who is that disturbing the peace?" The crowd grew quiet as the man who wore a gun and badge walked up to Lullaby.

I remember the look on Lullaby's face when the man stopped and stared at him. "You making all that noise?"

Lullaby face turned a pale white and he said, "yes sir."

"Good." the man said, "for I want to hear that song called *Barbara Allen.*"

Lullaby got his color back and started to play and sing. The man sat down and listened. When Lullaby finished the song, the man stood up, smiled, and said, "you folks have fun!" As he left, a sigh of relief went up from the crowd. They thought that big man was going to arrest Lullaby and put him in jail.

On the way back home Lullaby was quiet and everyone wondered what was the matter. The big man with the badge and gun had scared him.

There was a small church about a mile down the road from where we lived at the end of the bridge. Lullaby would pick up the people who lived on the farm and take them to church on Sunday. I remember that the church sat in a grove of trees and had benches among them. There would be certain Sundays when the people would bring food and have an all-day service with dinner. This particular Sunday was one of them. When we arrived at the church, we kids were put inside out of the way and the women began to set up the tables. After service was over the fun began. It was time to eat! The kids were given a plate and we went down to the big table and filled our plates. If you didn't get enough the first time there was always plenty for seconds.

When everyone was through eating, Lullaby picked up his guitar and everyone started singing. Someone in the crowd started to kid him about the incident with the deputy sheriff over in Kingston.

I will away remember what Lullaby said. "I thought that big man was going to take me to the rock pile. I would still be there singing *Barbara Allen* if he had wanted me to."

Gypsy

One day recently as I turned off Martha Berry Highway onto to John Davenport Drive, a memory came to me of something that happened when I lived there as a small child. We had moved from Kingston to a street in Rome called Wright Row. Wright Row ran from Martha Berry Highway and made a curve back up across the railroad. Wright Row was done away with when John Davenport Drive was put in. I can drive though the area and in my mind see it as it existed back then. At that time, Martha Berry was U.S Route 27. I remember there was a row of houses just as you came under the railroad underpass. Several sat facing the road and there were two or three that ran down the side of the railroad. These houses were on the right side of the road. A few feet past the underpass on the left, a dirt road ran down though what looked like woods. As you turned onto the road, there were no houses on the left, just woods, a short span of trees and then an open field. A big oak tree stood on the edge of the trees and under it was a huge spring of water. That was some of the coldest spring water that I ever drank.

As you turned down the road, a house sat up close to the railroad on the left side. That was where the old hermit lived, we were told. A grassy field separated the next house from the old hermit. There were three houses sitting close together and then, where the road turned to go back across the railroad tracks, were three more. As I remember, there were seven houses on Wright Row at that time.

My father started attending church at the Church of Christ on Fifth Avenue which was on the left side of the street going toward town. The week always ended with everyone getting up and eating breakfast together. After breakfast we all walked to church. After church we would walk back home. That was a long walk. This was the way that Sunday was spent.

We had no way of knowing that this particular Sunday would be different. We were all seated at the table and just beginning to eat when a loud knock sounded at the front door. My Father got up and went to the door with me behind him. When he opened the door Mrs. Dean, who lived in the first house close to the old hermit, was standing on the porch.

"Look Mister Adcock," she said pointing across the road.

I squeezed out past my Father onto the porch and I can remember getting the surprise of my life. There across the road in what was an open field was a row of wagons which had been placed in a round circle. A tent was being put up in front of the wagons. Smaller tents were placed among the wagons. Some horses were in the field and there was some hay stacked up. A fence of rope contained the horses. As best my memory serves me, the horses were all black.

"What kind of folks are they?" I heard Mrs. Dean ask.

My father replied, "Gypsies."

After a few more words, Mrs. Dean left and we went back to breakfast and then to church.

I remember that I could hardly wait to get back home and see the Gypsies. The rest of the day I sat on the porch and watched them putting up the tent and placing the wagons. It was hard to go to bed that night for the Gypsies kept on working after dark. The next morning found me on the porch staring in amazement at the Gypsy camp. I remember that it looked like a small town but no one was seen moving around. I must have stayed on the front porch most of the day. My sisters had gone to school so it was just me on the porch watching, but when they got home, they joined the watching. After supper it was back on the porch. Now there was music coming from the camp.

As it began to get dark, cars started to come and park on the road and people walked into the Gypsies' camp. It began to be a noisy place with the music and people combined. I occasionally heard a noise that sounded like someone kicking a drum. I found out later a board in the stage where the girl danced was made so it would make a noise when she kicked it. There was no electric power in that area back then. The people who lived in the houses on Wright Row had to use kerosene lamps. The Gypsies had set up poles and hung lanterns on them. Sitting on the porch and looking at them was quite a sight! We wanted to go over but our father would not let us. He promised that he would take us on the following Saturday. I remember thinking that Saturday would never come.

Saturday did come and we found ourselves going across the street and into the Gypsy camp. Looking back I realize that it was a small carnival without the rides. There were jewelry and all kinds of handmade leather goods for sale. There were tents with side shows and there was the dark haired, dark eyed dancing girl who kept stomping on a board in the floor of the stage to make the loud noise. At the foot of the stage, the man they called the Hermit stood talking to the girl who did the dancing. She went up on stage and began to dance. My father stopped and talked to Hermit for a few minutes. It wasn't too long before we went back to the house. I took up my position on the porch, but bedtime was called, so it was off to bed for me.

I was up early the next morning. I wanted to see the Gypsies. I ran to the front door and opened it, stopping in my tracks. I stepped out on the porch to get a better look. There was nothing to see for, as the Gypsies had come in the night, they had left the same way. The field was empty. Neither a Gypsy nor a wagon was anywhere to be seen.

Hermit

One of the first things the grownups told us kids after we moved to Wright Row was we were not to go in the old hermit's yard. I was so young I didn't know what a hermit was. I remember sitting at the edge of the field where we played and watching for the hermit. The man who lived in that house would come and go, but I never saw a hermit. It took me a while to understand that the people were calling the man who lived in the house a hermit. I remember his name was Jacob. Whether this was his first or last name I never knew.

Jacob was, as I remember, a tall slim person with a bushy head of hair. When we started going to church, we met Jacob and he and my Father became good friends. Every Sunday he was in church. I remember that he was always surrounded by a group of girls. Why the people who lived next to him called him a hermit I never understood. He was very popular among the girls and well liked by the older people. The people on Wright Row called him old, but he was probably in his early thirties. He was always well-dressed and drove a big black automobile that gleamed so brightly you could see yourself in it.

This Sunday began no differently than others. Get up, eat, and get ready for church. It would turn out to be different because Jacob did not show up in church. Service started and everyone looked back to where Jacob usually sat. The seat was empty; no Jacob could be seen. After service was over a committee was formed to check on him. The next Sunday the committee members reported that they talked to someone at Jacob's tobacco shop on Broad Street and learned that he was on vacation. That took care of the matter for the time being.

The next Sunday was about the same as the previous one had been. Everyone was seated and the place where Jacob usually sat was still vacant. Just as the preacher started to talk, the door opened. Everyone turned to see who had come in.

A quietness settled over the crowd as the preacher spoke. "Let us all welcome Brother Jacob and his new bride."

Everyone turned and looked at them. I climbed up in the bench so I could see. There in his usual place sat Jacob with his new bride, the dark-haired, dark-eyed Gypsy dancing girl!

Halloween

We moved from Wright Row to Armstrong Street in West Rome. Armstrong Street ran off Allen Street. As far as I know, Allen and Armstrong no longer exist. Allen Street ran from Division to the railroad tracks at what is now the other end of John Davenport. Armstrong ran along the switch track at the back of old Fairbanks. There were a lot of young boys living in the area. As I recall none of us ever got into serious trouble.

One Halloween people dressed in different costumes were going though the neighborhood. A friend of mine who lived in the house across the street from us came over and asked my mother if I could come over to his house. She agreed to let me go with the understanding that his house would be as far as I could go. We sat on the front porch and watched the people parading up and down the street. My friend's mother and father were sitting on the porch keeping an eye on us. As I recall we were having a good time but we could not see what was about to happen.

As I said, Armstrong Street ran along the switch track for the railroad. As most older people know, back then you had what were called outhouses for a bathroom. They usually sat back from the house so, cold or hot, you had to get out in the weather to use the outhouse. The outhouses for these houses on Armstrong sat close to the railroad switch track. On this particular Halloween, some of the boys in the neighborhood decided to have some fun and turn the outhouses over. They started at the first one and came all the way to the last one pushing them all over.

We were still on the front porch and had not noticed that my friend's father had gotten up and left. After a while my friend's mother told us to go and check on his father since he had been gone a long time. Getting a flashlight so we could see, we headed for the outhouse. When we got to where the outhouse was supposed to be, we didn't see it. It wasn't until we shone the light around that we saw it lying front down in the tall grass. We could hear a muffled cry coming from it.

"Daddy! Daddy!" my friend hollered, running over to the overturned outhouse.

"Get me out of here!" his father yelled.

We tried to turn it over but the two of us were not strong enough.

"Go get your mother and tell her to get some help and get me out of here!" he yelled at us.

We ran back to the house and my friend told his mother what had happened.

"Go get some of the neighbors to help us," she said.

We went to several houses and came back with the neighbors. We all trooped back to the overturned outhouse and they all helped right it. My friend's father crawled out, reached down pulled up his pants and headed straight for his house. He never looked at or spoke to anyone. You could see that he was too embarrassed. Nobody said anything as he went inside and shut the door. Everyone left, not saying anything about what had happened.

No one saw my friend's father for the next several days. I stopped on my way to school, but was told that he was not going. I would hurry home from school to see if he wanted to come out and play. Each time I was told that he couldn't; he had to stay inside. I came home from school about the middle of the week to find a truck backed up to his front porch. His family had loaded up everything in the house and were just getting in to leave. I looked for my friend but he had already left. It was many years later that I found out that they had moved to north Rome. The embarrassment that he had felt over the outhouse incident would not let him face his neighbors. He was a good man who had gotten caught up in a prank that was meant to do no harm. No one ever admitted to turning over the outhouses. I do not ever remember any thing like that ever happening again.

I would come home from school and look across the street in hope of seeing my friend there. The house remained empty for several weeks but one day when I got home from school there was a truck backed up to the porch. Someone was moving in. I sat down on the steps and watched as they carried furniture in the house. Someone called out a name and I heard a boy answer. I watched as he came out on the porch. I stared at him, for he was about my age. I heard the name Duggan called again. Some seventy years later Duggan and I are still friends.

Sack Fishing

During the Depression, we had no money to spend on the better things in life. We had to make things that help us with our chores and entertainment. For example, I did not have the money to buy fishing equipment, so I had to make my own. A friend and I came up with the idea to make us a net. We went up to a little store on Allen Street called Pruitt's. Mr. Pruitt gave us some potato sacks. They had holes in them that would let the water pour out. We made a loop out of clothesline wire and attached the top of the potato sack to it. Then we attached the whole thing to a stick, and there was our fishing net! We would run it though the creek water. We caught a lot of good sized fish that got trapped in pools when the creek was up. In those days the streams were clean. You could eat the fish that you caught.

One of the more memorable sack fishing incidents happened just after the creek had been out of its banks for several days. My friend, Reece, and I convinced our parents that the creek was down enough that if we fell in, it wasn't so deep that we could not get out. Reece had a brother who was older than we were. He ran ahead of us with a burlap sack, jumped in the water and caught all the fish. We tried to slip off from him and succeeded for a while. We had caught us a nice string of fish when we heard him coming down though the woods.

"There you are," he said. "Thought you could get away without me?"

"Go home," Reece said, "and leave us alone."

We could see that it wasn't going to do any good trying to get rid of him. He ran past us, jumped into a big hole of water and yelled, "There's a big one in here!"

We watched as he opened up the mouth of his sack and chased something in the water. He let out another yell. "Boy, have I got a big one this time!"

The creek bank was slippery from his splashing. He tried to scramble up while holding the sack, but each time he fell back in.

"Reece! Come get this sack where I can get out."

"No way!" retorted Reece.

He and I had enough fish so we were ready to quit anyway, so we sat and laughed while Reece's brother dragged himself and the sack out of the creek.

Whatever he had in the sack was a handful. He finally was able to sit down on a stump. Reece and I quit laughing and eyed the sack which was moving all over the ground. I remember looking down at my fish which were good-sized but not like whatever was moving that sack!

Reece's brother jumped up on the stump holding the sack and said, "The mighty fisherman Charles has struck again!" With that he grabbed the bottom of the sack and began to shake it.

Well, we were not prepared for what we saw! The head came out first and it was a big head, only it wasn't a fish head. Reece and backed off because the head that was coming out of the sack was a snake! I have seen some large snakes in the area but few as big as this one. He came out head first and looked as if he was looking at Charles, who let out one of the wildest yells I've ever heard. He hit the ground arunning. Wet and muddy clothes sure weren't holding him back. The snake took off after Charles.

Charles ran for a piece, stopped, and turned around looking for the snake. The snake seemed to sense what had happened and went slithering down the path toward him. Another yell and all we could see was Charles running and the snake behind him. I know nothing about snakes but I do know that it was following him. Reece and I didn't let any grass grow under our feet, either. We got out of there.

We got back to the street just in time to see Charles run in the house and shut the door. We looked around to see if the snake was still after him, but didn't see it anywhere. We walked on to Reece's house and stopped in the front yard.

"Mighty fisherman Charles! Come to the front door," hollered Reece. We waited. Reece hollered again. The door opened and Charles came out on the porch. Reece and I both started laughing again, which sent Charles back into the house.

I have often wondered whether the snake really did chase Charles, or was it simply trying to escape? Charles had caught it in the water so I would surmise that it was a water moccasin. Was that snake mad because he had been stuffed in a muddy sack? Be careful what you stuff in a sack for it just might backfire on you!

Kick the Can

I grew up in the thirties and forties. Money was hard to come by and those who had a good job a place to live, and food to eat were among the lucky ones. Shoes and clothes were thrown away only if completely worn out. Boy's pants had patches on patches. Shoes would have holes patched with cardboard. If you saw a kid playing with a store bought toy, you knew his parents were rich or held a high-level executive job. Most kids played some game that had been passed down by their parents, and relied on their imagination to invent games. Rolling an old tire or playing kick the can were common games. Tires you could roll year around.

Kick the Can was only played when you could wear your shoes. Toes and shins can't handle being kicked against a tin can. We would find old tin cans and beat the cut edges down to where they were safe. I've worked on the cut edges of a can with a hammer for many an hour smoothing all the edges out. A can with the edges properly smoothed out was a priceless toy.

A friend of mine, Raymond, who lived across the street from us, was my partner when we kicked the can in competition with other boys. We would take the can everywhere we went, kicking it along in front of us. In those days you could walk up the middle of a street kicking the can for there were few cars on the road. Raymond and I would kick the can up the road to Allen Street, then up Allen to Division Street.

There was a small store on Division called Swinford Grocery Store. One day we made it to the store and left the can on the front porch when we went inside. Raymond had his hands full when we came back out, so I picked up the can from the porch. We crossed the street and started toward the intersection of Division and Allen. There was a house that sat on the corner back in those days. The house had my view of the intersection blocked, but I gave the can one of my best kicks anyway. A better kick I had never made for the can sailed up and started its downward flight just as a truck pulled to a stop at the interjection. Back in those days men would buy a car and cut it down to make a truck out of it, and this is what this guy was driving. Just as the truck came to a stop, the can hit the glass with a loud crack. The driver's side door flew open and a big man jumped out, stared at me a minute, then inspected the glass in the back of the cab. I stood frozen. I knew that man was going to kill me for hitting the glass! He reached over and picked up the can, holding it aloft.

"Is this yours?" he asked.

"Yes sir," I whispered.

"Is this yours?" he asked again in a loud voice.

"Yes sir!" I spoke up in a stronger voice.

He started toward me holding the can. But he obviously saw my fright, so he stopped in front of me and smiled. "Did you kick that can all the way over there from here?" he said.

"Yes sir," I answered. "I was standing right here."

The man shook his head. "I used to kick the can when I was a boy but I don't recall ever kicking it that far!"

I relaxed and he put the can on the ground with the bottom end facing him. He drew back his foot and let go. The can sailed across the road and landed on top of a high bank.

"Not bad!" he said, "but not as good as your kick. Son, be careful with that can. It can be dangerous if kicked in a crowd." He got back in his truck and drove down Division Street toward Shorter Avenue.

I looked at the high bank and wondered how I was going to get my can. I turned and looked at Raymond who hadn't said a word the entire time, and then started to the bank and began to climb. It was a hard climb but I had lot of time invested in that can. I made it to the top and, with the can in hand, slid down the bank and headed home.

I had learned my lesson about kicking the can in the road. Raymond and I dug holes in the ground and put up sticks as markers. Then we would see how many kicks it took to make the course. The one with the less kicks became the champion. One day I would be champion and the next day Raymond would be. But there was one boy named Buddy who had us both beat. I would put everything I had into the game, but Buddy would still beat me. I kicked those cans a million miles or more back in my young days but the one thing the grown man in the cut down truck taught me was never kick that can into the road. Who knows what is coming around the corner?

Skinny Dipping

There was a small creek off Sherwood Road that ran behind the hill that Shorter College sits on. This creek ran under Horseleg Creek Road. At that time there was a dam there and that meant there was water in the old swim hole almost year round. It was nothing to find the swim hole full of young boys anytime the weather was hot. Most of the time the boys were skinny dipping. They would throw their clothes on the bank and jump in. There were never any girls at the swim hole because they all knew that the boys were skinny dipping. With no grown people and no girls around, it wasn't anything to see as many as eight or ten little naked butts splashing around in the water.

One day, unbeknownst to my mother, my friend Reece and I headed for the swim hole. It was like any other Sunday evening at the old swim hole full of naked boys. Not the first kind of swimsuit in sight. I sat down on a rock and hung my feet in the water and watched. I still had my clothes on for I had decided not to skinny dip this time. The hollers and laughter could be heard for quite a distance and it brought some girls from the college down to see what was going on. I was laughing at someone when a woman's voice said, "Be quiet and don't say a word!"

I turned to see four girls standing behind me. I yelled real loud and one of them pushed me off the rock into the water. There I sat looking at them with water up to my chin. I stood up, soaked to the skin. The girls began to gather up clothes from the bank and put them in a pile.

"Hey!" one of the boys yelled. "Those are our clothes!"

"Come and get them!" one of the girls taunted, holding up a pair of pants.

The boy started to stand up before he realized he didn't have on any clothes. "I can't do that!" he said squatting back down in the water.

"If you can't come up and show us what belongs to you, we're going to play Indian with them."

"Play what?" someone else asked.

"We are going to play Indian with your clothes!"

I didn't know what the girls were talking about when they said they would play Indian with the clothes. Then two of the girls began to gather sticks and put them in a pile that resembled a teepee. The clothes were stretched around the pile and covered it like the skins on a teepee. I watched, staying in the water making sure they didn't get my clothes to add to the teepee. I would say the girls were in their early twenties. I also realized that they were having themselves some fun.

Then one of the girls did something that I couldn't believe. She took a cigarette from a pack and began to smoke it. I must have been standing with my mouth open because she laughed and said, "Hey you with your bug catcher hanging open, shut it before it fills up with flies."

She pointed at me and said to one of the girls next to her, "That one acts like he never saw a woman smoke."

I shut my mouth when I realized she was talking about me. She was right! I had never seen a woman smoke a cigarette in my life. I watched as she laughed and blew smoke in the air.

One of the other girls walked over, lit up a cigarette and sat down on the rock where I had been sitting when they pushed me in to the water. I well remember her saying, "Sheril, look at the one with his clothes on. Let's pull him out and take them off him!"

A red-headed girl came over to the rock and pointed to me. "You bring them clothes to me or I'll come in and get them!"

I started to back up toward the bank on the other side. Then, to the amazement of all us boys, she undid a button on the side of the skirt she was wearing and pulled the skirt off! I thought I was looking at her underclothes, but it was only a pair of shorts that went with the skirt. Being a small boy, I had seen enough to move on. Move I did! When the redheaded gal's feet hit the water, I was climbing up the other bank. I didn't stop to look back until I was crossing Shorter Avenue. I got home dripping water with mud on my clothes. I took my punishment and never said a word about where I had been and what had happened.

I learned from Reece that the girls had a good laugh at my expense and left a short time later. They set the wood on fire and acted like Indians on the war path. They finally threw all of the clothes in the water and left. I know that they were students from Shorter who had some fun by making a bunch of small boys think they were going to burn their clothes. I know when that redheaded girl started to strip down to her underclothes, this little boy didn't stay around to see what was going to happen. That was the last time this boy ever went to that swimming hole!

left to right:
Duke Hughes,
Jimmy Chapman,
Lonie

First Hug

Small boys don't like girls and I was no different than other boys back then. (If I remember correctly, as I grew up, my thoughts on the matter changed.) The way my first hug came about is not what you would think. I had a sister who was five years older than I was. She had what us small boys called big girl friends. Now, back then there wasn't much to do in the way of entertainment. There wasn't enough money for the movies. My mother was from the old school where the people had to make their own entertainment. They told stories which were handed down from generation to generation. Most of these stories were ghost-related.

My mother could tell you ghost stories that would make the hair stand up on the back of your neck and chill bumps run up and down your spine. One warm night my sister had some of her friends at the house. They kept on at my mother to tell a ghost story. After a while she gave in and we all went out on the front porch. My mother sat in a rocker and the girls gathered around her on the floor. One of the girls, Lou, sat on the steps. My mother started to tell the one about the ghost who haunted a hallway in a big house. When you walked though the hall, this ghost would reach out and grab your arm.

I had heard this story and knew what was coming. I eased though the door and into the house. I crawled to the back door so no one could see me, went out and ran to the side of the house and crawled underneath the floor. Keeping as quiet as possible, I crawled to where Lou was sitting on the steps. I could see her foot resting on the step. I eased myself around to where I could see her leg. The girls were spellbound by the story my mother was telling. I listened and when my mother said, "and then the ghost reached out and grabbed her!" I reached up between the steps and grabbed Lou's leg. I shook it really hard and then scooted back under the porch. Lou let out a yell that could be heard for blocks.

I scurried back though the house without anyone knowing that I had even left the porch. Lou was standing behind my mother, shaking. It took a few minutes for her to calm down and tell what had happened.

My mother said, "Lonie, get that flashlight and bring it to me."

I did as I was told. She took the light and began to search under and around the house. I knew they wouldn't find anything, but I helped them look. I wanted to laugh but knew better, for if my mother had found out that I was the one who had grabbed Lou's leg, she would have tanned my hide. Finally satisfied that there was nothing around to hurt them, the girls decided to go home.

After they left, my mother and I went into the house. She was still puzzled as to what had happened. I went into the kitchen to get something to eat. She came in and sat down across the table from me. I knew then that she knew I had done the grabbing, but I wasn't going to let on. But then I made a mistake. I spoke. "I bet it was that old ghost that grabbed Lou by the leg."

She looked at me and I knew that I might as well say it.

"Lonie," she said, "that was you, wasn't it?"

I quit eating and dropped my head. I knew she had me. "Yes Mama, it was me."

She stood and looked at me and said, "You ought to be ashamed of yourself. Tomorrow you will go to Lou and tell her you are sorry for what you have done."

"Yes ma'am," I said, but the thought of going to Lou and admitting it was me who grabbed her leg didn't sit so well with me.

The next morning there wasn't much conversation directed my way. My sister had scolded me for scaring her friend. After breakfast, my mother and I headed to Lou's house. When we got there I had to stay on the front porch and wait while my mother went inside and talked to Lou. I was finally called inside to face Lou. I can't remember any thing in my life any harder than facing her. She was standing in the center of the room and my Mother motioned for me to go over to her. I can remember it as if it was yesterday. I know now that this little boy's heart was broken for what he had done.

With a tear in my eye I went over to Lou, dropped my head and mumbled, "I'm sorry for scaring you."

I will never forget how she put her hands on my shoulders and said, "I ought to be mad at you, but I'm not!" And then she bent down and hugged me. She actually put her arms around me and hugged me. I couldn't believe a girl had hugged me!

We left Lou's house and started back home. I knew if it got out that a girl had hugged me, I would be ragged. The gossip did get out and all my buddies kidded me. You would think that this would have taught me a lesson about leg grabbing. It didn't. I was known as a very mischievous person. Not mean, just mischievous. I knew that the hug Lou gave me was her way of saying she wasn't mad at me. I also learned that day that a hug wasn't a bad thing to have. In fact, I learned to like a good hug; still do.

If you want to give an old man a warm feeling, give him a big hug.

left to right: Julian, Wesley, and Lonie with their mother

Bully

Recently I saw a news segment on TV about a person being bullied. This brought back a memory of when I was in the third grade at Elm Street School in West Rome in the late 1930s.

All the kids in the third grade were small. A boy who had missed several grades and was in the fifth grade made it a habit to pick on all the smaller kids. His name was Milt, he was about fourteen and big for his age. He knew that if he waited until the small kids were off the school grounds, the school would not do anything about his bullying. There was a vacant lot at the corner of Elm and Shorter where the drug store is now. In the middle of this lot was a trail that the kids used for a short cut. It was here where Milt would do most of his bullying.

On this particular day, a friend named Billy and I were about in the middle of the lot when out of nowhere came Milt and shoved the palm of his hand between Billy's shoulders. Billy's books went flying in the air and he landed flat on his face.

I ran to where he had fallen. "Billy, are you hurt?"

He lay still.

Again I asked, "Are you hurt?" I turned him over. His face was a sight to see. Blood was running down it and he had dirt and grime all over him.

Milt ran over and jerked Billy to his feet saying, "Want some more?"

Little Billy, who was not half Milt's size, stood there crying and shaking, too scared to say anything.

I yelled, "Leave him alone!"

Milt turned on me. On several occasions in the past, Milt had shoved me and called me a papoose. Now, he shoved me backward and said, "Papoose, here tomorrow you'll get some of what he got!" Laughing he turned and ran down Shorter Avenue.

I helped Billy get his books and we went down to Hill Street, which is a church parking lot now. A small store was there. I believe it was called Caldwell Grocery. A lady who ran the store got Billy a wet cloth to clean his face. All the way home I kept hearing Milt say, "Papoose you get yours tomorrow!"

When I got home, I went inside. My mother said, "Where have you been? You're late."

I told her what had happened, leaving out the part about papoose. Then I told my mother I was going to play with a friend. Instead, I got a small hatchet and went to the woods along the railroad tracks. I cut myself the perfect stick. I then went back to the vacant lot and placed the stick in a clump of grass, making sure that I would know where it was the next day. I then went back home.

I didn't sleep much that night but was up ready to go to school the next morning. That walk to school was the longest I had ever been on, for with each step my feet got heavier and heavier. When I walked onto the school grounds, Milt saw me and walked over.

"Today, Papoose, is your day!" He laughed and ran into the schoolhouse.

Needless to say this didn't help to make my day.

The day seemed to go faster than usual and before I knew it school was out. I started across the vacant lot along with a group of kids. I was trying to keep my eyes open for Milt. I never saw him coming, though, because he had run up behind me and slapped me down before I even knew he was there. I remember crawling to where the stick was before he grabbed me from behind and threw me down on the ground. I was lying on my back. I reached out and grabbed the stick just as he bent over to hit me again. I remember hearing a loud thump as the stick hit him on the head. He let out a yell and I scrambled to my feet swinging the stick. I could tell that I was connecting with each swing. Milt started to run back toward the school with me behind him swinging the stick as hard and as fast as I could. The doors were open and he ran though them into the hall. I was on his heels still swinging the stick. He was yelling for the world to hear him. The teachers came out into the hall to see what was happening.

I have often wondered about what they must have felt when they saw the school bully screaming and running away from a small terrified boy. I backed Milt up against a wall and was still swinging the stick when a voice that was so familiar said, "Lonie Burt, give me the stick."

I remember that my nose was bleeding and my eye was almost swollen shut. A tug on the stick made me hold on tighter. The second time she called my name, I realized what was happening and turned loose the stick. My teacher led me to a chair and brought me a wet rag to wash my face. She placed a cold rag on my nose and said, "Hold this."

I looked around, but she had gone out in the hall where the others were. After a short time, my nose stopped bleeding but I was having a hard time seeing out of my left eye. My teacher came back with the principal and they stood in the door and talked. I couldn't hear what they were saying.

"Are you all right now?"

"Yes ma'am," I answered.

"Come," she said. "I'll take you home."

I got in her car and she pulled out of the school yard. I remembered my books were still scattered in the vacant lot. She stopped to let me collect them and when we got to my house, she got out and went to the door with me. She explained what had happened to my mother and gave her a letter.

When my teacher left, I asked my mother if I was in trouble. My father got home a while later and my mother gave him the letter. He read it, then asked me, "Did you start this with this boy?"

I assured my father that it was none of my doings and asked if I was in trouble. He looked at me with a look on his face that I had never seen before.

"No," he said, "but someone is!"

The next morning I had trouble seeing out of my left eye and my lid was swollen. My father and I headed for the school where we were shown into the principal's office. Billy's mother had brought him to the meeting as well. His face was all messed up. The principal explained since we boys had brought the fight back onto school grounds, the school would have to take action.

My father started to talk. What he said I was too small to understand. The room was quiet except for his voice. My father had been an evangelist preacher and had travelled all over this country for the church. He knew how to get people's attention.

"Burt," my father said, "you and Billy stand up here in front of us."

We got up and moved to where he had pointed.

"Now you," he pointed to Milt, "stand beside them."

Milt's father said, "Stand up there with them."

"Now," my Father said. "Look at the size of Burt and Billy and tell me that either one of them would be justified in using a stick to defend themselves against someone twice their size."

Milt's father stood up and said, "Milt has been nothing but a troublemaker since he started to school. No punishment is necessary for this. I'll take Milt out of school here and put him in an academy for troublemakers. There he will be disciplined and made to obey the academy rules."

The adults talked for a few more minutes. Billy and I were told that we could go to class. Milt was standing by the door. As we passed him, I heard him mutter, "Papoose!"

Billy and I went back to our class, glad to get out of there. When we opened the door and walked in, everyone in the room was looking at us. Our teacher just smiled and motioned for us to be seated.

As the years passed this incident was forgotten. But seeing the news about bullying brought it all back. I'm sure that there are still some people from that class who remember a small boy wearing overalls and a bowl hair cut chasing big Milt with a stick. President Teddy Roosevelt's saying "walk softly and carry a big stick" has a lot of truth in it. I've added an afterthought: Walk softly and carry a big stick and be willing to use it should the occasion arise.

Glue Britches

I was talking to a friend who had been reading one of my articles. He shook his head and said, "You must have been into everything that came along back when you were growing up!"

I don't recall ever starting trouble with anyone, but when trouble came to me, I would usually stand up and try to face the situation. As the old saying goes, "boys will be boys." I have always considered myself one hundred and ten percent all-American male. I never went out looking for trouble but never ran from it, either, when I found myself face to face with it.

I went to school at Elm Street with a boy named Herman. He was always doing something to someone to start a fight. He didn't always come out on top, but it didn't matter for he would be back the next day doing something to someone else. In those days, all the kids carried their lunch in a brown paper bag. As you entered the classroom, there was what we called a cloak room. You hung up your coats here and placed your lunch on a table that was put in the corner of the room for that purpose. Students wrote their names on their lunch bags. Most of the time, my lunch consisted of a biscuit with jelly. To have peanut butter and soda crackers was a treat.

On this particular day I had peanut butter and soda crackers and I could hardly wait until lunchtime to eat them. Finally, the lunch bell rang and everyone went to the cloak room to get their lunch. All morning I had been tasting my crackers and peanut butter. But upon entering the cloak room, I stopped short. My lunch was gone! I noticed a girl named Doris pointing toward a coat hanging by the door. I pulled the coat back and there, sitting on the floor eating my peanut butter and crackers, was Herman. He had taken all the crackers out of the bag and thrown the bag on the floor. He had almost finished one and held the others in his hand. I remember jumping on top of him and then my mind went blank.

When I realized what was happening, someone was holding me. I was being held up off the ground, my feet swinging in the air. A very stern voice said, "Lonie, you settle down this minute or I'll send you home!"

I felt my feet touch the floor and I stood still.

"Now young man," my teacher said, "tell me what happened."

"Herman got my lunch and was eating it!" I grew quiet for I knew that if I got sent home for fighting in school, a dusting of the seat of my pants would be waiting on me.

"Herman, what have you got to say about that? Did you take his lunch?"

"Yes," replied Herman, "I took his old peanut buttered crackers."

"You knew they weren't yours. Why did you take them?"

"I was hungry and didn't think he would do anything about it."

"It seems you were wrong. By the look of you, he did something about it."

My teacher went to her desk and brought out a sandwich which she gave to me. "Run on outside and eat," she said.

I turned to leave and I saw her grab Herman by the arm. "Not you, young man. I want to talk to you!"

Anyone who went to Elm Street School at that time knew she was not going to talk to him. This teacher was known to all the kids as the whipping teacher!

Herman quieted down for a while but soon he was back up to his old tricks. On one of those cold, rainy, winter days when the weather is not fit for man nor beast, we were having our recess inside. That day I had biscuits and jelly in my brown bag. I downed several biscuits full of jelly and developed a big thirst. I went out in the hall to get a drink of water. I had started back to the room when the door opened and a girl came out.

Herman put glue in your desk," she informed me in a whisper.

Herman sat in the desk beside me. When I got to my desk I saw the glue in the seat. Herman never knew what hit him. Before he knew it, I had *him* in the glue! I sat down on top of him where he couldn't move.

He began to whimper. "Let me up before the glue sets up!"

I held on for dear life and he stop squirming for he knew I had him.

Someone yelled, "Teacher!" I jumped up and ran around the room to the front. The door opened and the teacher came in. I asked her would she make Herman get out of my desk.

"Herman," she said, "get out of Lonie's desk."

"I can't!" he cried.

She headed to the desk to see why he couldn't get up. She stood with an amazed look on her face. I was standing behind her trying not to laugh.

"How did the glue get in the seat of the desk?" she asked.

Herman replied with a whimper, "I did it."

"You put the glue in the desk and then sat in it?"

I moved around to where I could look him in the face. I shook my head and he whimpered again. She gathered all of my books and stuff from the desk and told me to sit in a desk up front.

I remember that the janitor came and took the desk loose from the floor and, with Herman still in it, dragged it out into the hall. The teacher came back in the room and looked around until her eyes came to rest on me. I couldn't help it for I know that I had a smile on my face that stretched from ear to ear. Nothing was ever done about the glue. What had happened to Herman? You would think that Herman had learned a lesson but he didn't for in a few days he was back to his old tricks again.

Wee Wee Bush

In the early 1940s, I was living on Armstrong Street in West Rome. There was a woman who lived down the street who always gave me the idea that she was so much better than most folks. She drew a check from the government each month, so she was one of the few who had money. Most of the people who lived in the area were poor but happy. Everyone got along and as a rule better neighbors couldn't be found. If anyone needed a helping hand some were always willing to help.

I was a small boy at that time and even today can't understand her dislike of me. Now, in those days, no kid talked back to an older person no matter what the problem was. If I had talked back to a grown up, the seat of my pants would have been dusted off. I say no kid talked back to a grown person, but there was one who did—her son. The lady had a boy about my age who didn't listen to anything his mother said. It seemed to me that she took it out on me and not her boy. I never told my Mother about her and things she said and did to me. If I had told my mother, there would have been, as the saying goes, hell to pay.

I played with her boy and got along with him. We would pitch ball to each other for hours at a time. At that time we both wanted to be baseball players as boys still do. I remember a time when we were playing pitch in his front yard and she came out and told me to get out of her yard. I did and her boy followed me home. We played in my yard. I never went back in her yard again except for the time she asked me to.

One day I watched a man back a truck up in her yard and unload some bushes. There were four of them. I can remember it as if it was yesterday instead of so long ago. I passed by going to the store for my mother and wondered about the bushes. On my way home, she called out to me. I looked at her, wondering what she wanted. This was the first time she ever called out to me.

She pointed at me and said, "Come here, Adcock." She never called me by my first name, only by my last.

I hesitated, not understanding what was happening to make her call me. I hesitantly walked up in the yard.

"Yes ma'am," I said. "Did you want me?"

"See those bushes?" she said, pointing to them.

"Yes ma'am," I said.

"I will give you two dollars if you'll dig holes for those bushes. Can you do that?"

"Yes ma'am. Let me take this home to my mother and I will be back."

I ran home as fast as I could and told my mother what I was going to do. I didn't tell her how much money she said she would pay. My father had passed away a few months prior to this and things were tough around my house. I knew that two dollars would buy a lot of groceries. I practically ran back so I could get started digging those holes. She was waiting for me and had placed a brick where she wanted the holes dug. I want you to imagine a little skinny eleven year old boy swinging a man-sized pick in rough, hard-packed dirt. It was hot, but I kept at it and finally I had all four holes dug. I went up and knocked on the door and she came and looked out.

"What?" she asked. "You don't think that you are through?"

"Yes ma'am," I replied. "All the holes are dug deep enough to put the bushes in."

"Well, put them in the holes and plant them!" She slammed the door.

I looked at my hands which were full of blisters and bleeding. I remembered she had said dig the holes. Not once was anything was said about me planting the bushes. I knew that I wouldn't get my two dollars if I didn't plant them, so I got a bucket of water and began to put the bushes in the holes. I had been almost all day digging the holes and now I was having to plant those bushes. Finally I got them planted and again knocked on her door.

She came out but didn't say anything as she began to look at the bushes. As she started back into the house, she said, "Wait and I will get you your money."

It took her a few minutes. She came back out and handed me a dollar.

I wouldn't take it. "You told me you would give me two dollars."

"You, Adcock," she said, "will take this dollar because that is all you get." She threw the dollar at me and turned to go inside. From her porch, she said, "Get out of my yard or I will call the police to you!" She slammed the door and once again yelled, "Adcock, get out of my yard."

I picked up the dollar in my bleeding hands and left. There was a field across the road from her house so I went over and sat down against a tree. You can imagine what an eleven year old boy who had a broken heart did. The tears rolled down my cheeks. I had my heart set on giving my mother those two dollars to buy groceries. After the hurt dried up and the anger took over, I began to wonder what I could do to get even. I stood up and started back across the street with the intent to pull the bushes out of the ground.

Just as I got to the edge of her yard, the door flew open and she came out on the porch.

"I want my dollar!" I said to her.

"I'm calling the police to you now!" she exclaimed.

I went home knowing that it would do no good to get myself in trouble with her. I gave the dollar to my mother and began to doctor my hands. I knew that it would be a few days before I would pitch any ball. My mother questioned me to see if there had been any problem with the woman. I let on that every thing was okay.

After supper I went out on the front porch and sat down in a swing. I was so tired that I fell asleep. My mother woke me up when it was dark and told me to go on to bed. I started around the house to use the outhouse. That's when the idea struck me. In those days, there were no street lights to light up the streets. It was dark and no one could see you until they got up close.

I turned and headed for the freshly planted bushes. I began to wee wee first around the roots, then on the leaves. I only had enough wee wee for two bushes. I hurried back home and got into bed. No one had seen me, so I was safe. And I was able to "water" the bushes regularly!

I kept watch on the two bushes that had been watered with wee wee. The first thing I noticed was that the leaves began to turn yellow. The other two bushes had begun to bloom, but there were no blooms on the wee wee bushes. They began to look dead. Dead they were for she paid a man to bring in two more bushes and plant them in the holes where the others had died. It was odd for if I remember those two bushes put on a bloom and began to look real pretty. Then a strange thing happened. The new bushes also began to turn yellow and the leaves and blooms fell off. While we lived there I know that lady replaced those two bushes several times. They would begin to look real pretty and all of a sudden they would die.

As I write this, I know that two wrongs do not make a right. What that lady did to me was not right. What I did to her was not right. You know the old saying "what goes around, comes around."

I will say that she got payback for doing what she did to a small boy. Anyone will tell you payback is hell. I'll also give you this advice: don't water your bushes with wee wee!

Play Ball

When I was a kid, we played ball in a field close to our house on Armstrong Street. One day a fellow I'll call Ben saw us kids playing. He told us if we practiced and got good enough he would get us some games with different teams. Ben brought us a bat and gloves so we would have equipment to play with. He would come by and watch us and say, "Not good enough, keep practicing!" We practiced and we practiced some more. We played enough ball that year to do me the rest of my life.

One Friday Ben came by and said he had lined up a game for the next day.

"Who do we play?" we asked.

He smiled and replied, "Snake Island."

"Snake Island? Where's that?" I asked.

At the time of this ball game, Snake Island could have been an island somewhere in the ocean as far as we knew, but we soon learned that Snake Island was in East Rome. It was the area around the railroad track there on East Twelfth at Anchor Rome. Old Anchor Rome was a cotton mill that stood where the new Health Department is now. The boys on Snake Island were supposed to be mean. But all of the players on my team were fired up and ready to play.

I woke up early on Saturday, ready for the big game. I put on my clothes, ate a fast breakfast and went out to where the others were waiting. Ben came by and said for us to practice until he came back for us. Practice we did, over and over until we gave out. We had begun to think he wasn't coming back for us when he finally pulled up driving his pickup truck. We loaded in the back and he pulled onto Allen Street headed toward Division, turned down Division Street going toward the railroad and pulled into an open field where the new Willingham Village is now. There was nothing around except a pile of sawdust where some logs had been cut. Ben and some of the other men had laid off a baseball field with something that left white lines on the ground. It looked good to us because we had never played on a field that was drawn off. The bases were made of flour sacks full of sand.

"Oh boy," I remember saying to one of the boys, "this is just like they do in the movies!"

Then a pickup truck full of boys pulled in. Ben said, "Boys, there's the Snake Island team."

We watched as they unloaded from the truck. I realized that what I first thought were uniforms was nothing but everyone of them wearing the same kind of clothing. It sure looked like baseball uniforms. I also noticed the Snake Island boys were a lot bigger than we were. That didn't sour our spirits any for we were ready to play ball! Ben and another man got us all together and gave us a talk about playing fair and according to the rules. They then tossed a coin to see who was first at bat. We won and took our positions. I remember looking at the Snake Island team and how neat they looked and how ragtag we looked. Our team wore everything from overalls to coveralls.

"Play ball! Batter up!" yelled the referee.

The first batter up was short and sweet for he swung three times and was out. This is what happened for us the first two or three times we were at bat. Then they scored several runs. I watched the pitcher. As he wound up to throw the ball, he would put his hands above his head, wiggle them and stick out his tongue. This would cause the batter to look at him instead of the ball so that when he swung, the ball was already gone by. I asked Ben if he could do this and Ben replied that he wasn't breaking any rules. I watched the finger wiggling and the tongue thing and decided that when it came my time to bat, I would ignore it and concentrate on the ball.

I stepped up to the plate swinging the bat back and forth the way

I had seen them do in the movies. I stood there in my overalls and waited for the pitcher to throw the ball. (I found out later that his name was Homer.) Well, Homer threw the ball and it came at me like a bullet. I swung and missed. I realized that I had been watching him do his hand thing. I remember saying to myself, "Not this time, Homer old boy!" The ball left his hand, coming straight at me. I mustered up all the power that was in me and just as the ball got to me, I swung. I heard the crack as the bat hit the ball and felt it all over my body. I dropped the bat and ran. First base, second base, and finally third! I had made them all! Then I realized that something was wrong. All the people were on the pitcher's mound. I watched as they picked Homer up and placed him on the tailgate of a pickup truck. I walked out to where Homer was now sitting up. There between his eyes was a lump as big as a baseball.

He looked at me and said, "Good shot!"

As much as he was hurting, I could tell that he wasn't mad at me. "I didn't mean to hurt you!"

With some help he got down off of the tailgate and was put in a car and taken to the hospital.

I found out later from Ben that he was all right. There were no serious effects from being smacked between the eyes by my hit. I also learned from Homer himself years later that when he threw the ball and raised his hand to his head for what he called his ritual, that was when the ball smacked him. He said he saw it coming and tried to duck, but didn't make it. He told me he never played another ball game. I never threw another ball at a game, but I did practice throwing for different reasons.

I shall always remember the ragtag Allen Street team playing the good looking Snake Island team. I'll always remember Homer with the knot between his eyes too.

Toothbrush

While at the dentist talking to the lady who cleaned my teeth, the subject of brushing came up. I brought up the subject of tooth brushes by telling her that when I was growing up money was scarce and what little you had you didn't spend on toothbrushes and paste. I remember that I laughed, saying I didn't know what toothpaste was until I was almost grown.

She looked surprised. "If you didn't brush, how have you managed to keep your teeth all these years?"

I explained that we brushed, but not with the type of toothbrushes she was familiar with. When we were growing up, we went into the woods with our mother and cut small limbs from a sweet gum tree. We would peel the bark from them and chew until that got soft like today's toothbrushes. Mother would mix baking soda and salt and we would brush our teeth with it. She would see to it that we brushed with the mixture after each meal we ate.

We kids had our mixture, but our mother had another one that she used. Her mixture was snuff. I would sit and watch her and she seemed to enjoy it. Now the soda and salt wasn't the best tasting thing in the world. I wondered why she wouldn't let me use snuff instead of the soda and salt. She kept her snuff in a small box on a high shelf so we kids couldn't get to it.

One day I decided that I knew how to get that snuff. I pulled a chair up to the cabinet, climbed on top of the counter, and from there stood up and opened the top door where she kept her snuff. It worked! When she wasn't looking, I got the small box of snuff and headed around the house out of sight. I sat down and leaned back against the house and took out my toothbrush. I wet it and put the end into the box of snuff, then put the brush in my mouth. Wow, was it good! It was sweet and I took a big swallow. When I say swallow, I mean I swallowed the mouthful of fluid that the snuff created. It was a big mouthful and as it went down, I felt the effects of the snuff. The juice may have been sweet-tasting, but when it hit the bottom of my stomach, it had a nausea effect. I began to vomit. I remember sitting against the side of the house with my legs spread apart and my insides coming up.

By this time, my mother had missed me so she told my sister to find me. When she found me vomiting, she got scared and ran and got my mother. It didn't take long for our mother to see what had happened. I remember the look on her face and saying to myself, "you've had it now!"

She and my sister toted me into the house and put me on a sofa. I lay still, afraid that if I moved my stomach would act up again. I had never been as sick as I was that day. Needless to say I didn't eat any supper! Did I learn a lesson from this? Maybe!

I had a half brother who had a farm in Bartow County and he and my father grew tobacco on it. They would dry it and make it into cigars and chewing tobacco. After supper my father would go out on the front porch and smoke a homemade cigar. They smelled good, like maple syrup. I didn't know it then, but they used maple syrup in the making of the cigars. I would sit on the steps and smell the smoke and want to take a puff from the cigar, but I knew what would happen if I were caught smoking. The seat of my pants would get a dusting!

I remember well one particular evening. My father lit up his cigar and I sat on the steps smelling the smoke. It smelled so good that I could hardly wait for him to throw the butt down. I had made my mind up that I was going to get it and have myself a few puffs. I waited patiently and finally he threw the cigar butt in the yard before going inside. I waited until he was out of sight, then grabbed the cigar and around the house I went. I cleaned off the end of the cigar and took myself a big puff. I started to cough but the sweet taste of the cigar got to me. I swallowed a mouthful of juice from the cigar. It tasted funny, but I had another puff. I coughed again, again but down went the sweet juice into my stomach. I looked at the cigar for it was beginning not to taste so good. I remember thinking, *I'll try one more puff to see if it's any better.*

I never made it to that final puff for everything I had for supper came up right back up. The vomit covered me and my surroundings! I didn't know that my father had been watching me through the window. When I vomited up my supper, he came around the house and got me. The next thing that I knew, I was on the sofa with a wet cloth on my forehead. He told my mother that I would be all right and maybe I had learned a lesson.

Later, when I first went on the police force, I worked with a policeman who chewed tobacco. I would see him bite off a chew from a plug of tobacco, but would never see him spit. I asked him one day if he swallowed the juice from the tobacco. He smiled and said yes, it keeps me from having worms. I knew he was kidding and am sure he didn't have worms. I don't believe worms could survive the tobacco juice!

If you get worms, see your doctor for if you try to kill them with tobacco juice, you're in for a surprise. I did learn my lesson about tobacco from those childhood incidents. I learned if you dip, chew or puff, don't swallow the juice! Spit, spit and then spit some more!

Bush Arbor

One morning, my friend Raymond came to our house on Armstrong Street and said, "Lonie, come outside and see what's happening."

I ran out to where he was and he pointed to the field which was vacant except for a truck and some men unloading posts from it.

"What are they doing?" I asked him.

"Don't know. They just got here."

"Come on," I said going to where I could get a good look.

Raymond and I sat down with our backs against a tree and watched. The men began to dig holes and set the posts in them. Before long before they started to lay a frame for the top. A truck pulled in loaded with what looked like tree limbs. They began to spread the limbs across the top. In no time at all they had what is called a bush arbor. I know that there are some people who know what a bush arbor is and some who do not. At the end close to the road, the men made a platform that was about a foot off the ground. This was floored and a top that looked like a tent was stretched across it. The men then began to bring in sacks of sawdust and spread it over the ground under the arbor. A podium was brought in and placed on the platform. Raymond and I watched in amazement at how fast they had put the arbor up. The arbor finished, they then took a big sign from the truck and set it facing the road. When the men finished, they loaded onto the trucks and left. Now, being the nosy kind that we were, Raymond and I had to see what was on the sign. Were we in for a surprise!

There, stretching from the top of the sign to the bottom, was a picture of a skinny man. Standing beside him was a woman who was as big around as she was tall. As close as I can remember, the sign read:

Bush Arbor Revival
Come hear the gospel according to Brother John Ramsey
Hear the beautiful voice of Sister Etta
Starting this Sunday and running for a week

Raymond and I went on home talking about going to see the tall skinny man. Come Sunday night Raymond and I were sitting out front next to the platform. The tall skinny man came out to the podium and began to talk. We sat there spellbound for as skinny as he was, he had a deep bass voice. He would walk the platform back and forth as he talked. Once he dropped a paper from his Bible and without bending his knees he reached down and picked it up. He had the longest arms that I had ever seen on anyone. Sister Etta sat in a chair behind him, along with two men who had guitars.

He walked, he talked, and finally said, "Now we will hear the beautiful voice of Sister Etta!"

Sister Etta moved to the front of the platform along with the men and their guitars. The men began to pick the guitars and what came next was a surprise to all. Sister Etta began to sing and sing she did. I have never heard a voice even today that was as beautiful. She held the people spellbound with her singing. Then she stopped singing and the skinny man began to talk again.

It was this way for the rest of the week with Raymond and me sitting down front listening. On Saturday night the skinny man made the announcement that Sunday would end the revival and to wear appropriate clothing for the altar. We had no idea what he meant by appropriate clothes or what an altar was.

Sunday night found Raymond and me sitting in our favorite position with our backs against the post at the edge of the platform. The platform had been covered with a floor covering like that used in a gym. We sat down and watched the people as they came in bringing their chairs with them. Strangely all the women wore long dresses. I asked Raymond if he knew why the women wore long dresses. He didn't have an answer, so we sat and waited for the service to start.

Start it did. From out of nowhere the skinny man hit the platform talking in a language that I didn't understand. The people started to move up on the platform until it was full. The tall man continued to jump around and yell in a voice that I could not understand. He took a stocking-like object from the podium, turned and hit a man in the head with it. A powder-like substance came from the stocking as it struck the man's head. A lady who lived across the street stood shouting something that I didn't understand. It must have made the skinny man mad because he turned and struck her on the head with the stocking thing. A man standing close to her caught her, lowering her to the floor. Now try to picture in your mind what this looked like to two small boys.

Amid all the noise Raymond whispered, "He killed her!"

I watched to see if she was dead. She certainly didn't move. The tall skinny man came over and without bending his knees clasped her head in one hand, reached up with the other hand toward the top of the arbor and shouted. He then shook her head and a moan came from her.

My feet were beginning to get a little restless by now. Then the woman threw her hand out striking my foot. This didn't help matters any. My feet really began to want to move! Then she rolled over on her side. I looked but couldn't see any eyes, only white spots. I know now that she had her eyes rolled back in her head, but I didn't know that then! This only made matters worse. To top it all off, she grabbed my foot. She shook it like it was a rag and let out a yell of some sort. That did it! I went sliding around that post and hit the ground running. I forgot about Raymond. As I made it to my porch, I heard the door across the street slam. Raymond had been in front of me. I went running though the front door.

My mother said, "Slow down! What's the matter with you?"

"That man, he killed that woman!" I replied, all out of breath. I went on to tell my mother about the lady getting hit in the head with the stocking thing, getting knocked down, and how the skinny guy had squeezed her head making her lose her eyes.

My mother assured me that he had not killed the woman and sent me off to bed. I went, but I didn't sleep much that night.

The next day my mother sent me to the Pruitt Grocery store just past the switch track on Allen Street. I went up Armstrong to Allen and started toward the store. Suddenly I stopped dead in my tracks. Coming down the street with a bag of groceries was the woman that the tall man had killed! I crossed to the other side of the street and watched as she went by. She seemed to be all right but last night she sure had looked dead lying there stretched out on the platform. I watched until she went in to her house and then crossed back over to the other side. I went on to the store and once inside Mister Pruitt asked me what would I have. I couldn't remember what I had come to the store for!

Ride It Cowboy

Like all young boys, at one time I wanted to be a cowboy. We would go to the movies and see Buck Jones, Wild Bill Elliot or maybe Roy and Gene round up the bad guys. They always rode a very smart horse, which I thought was the most beautiful thing in the world. But sometimes things happen that will spoil the best of dreams. This happened to me in the early forties and changed my whole outlook on riding a horse of any kind.

My sister and I would go up to Bartow County and spend time with my half brother and his family. He had a large family and to go stay with them for a few days was like having a vacation. He had a boy who was close to my age named Weldon. As soon as my sister and I arrived, Weldon and I would head for the woods to play Cowboys and Indians. My half brother had a horse that he used to plow with. One day Weldon and I went up to the pasture and decided that we had ridden stick horses long enough. We were going to ride the real thing, old Tobey! We climbed on top of the gate and waited for Tobey, but he wouldn't come anywhere near us.

"You stay here," Weldon told me, "and I'll go get him and come back for you."

I sat on the top of the gate and watched as Weldon caught old Tobey and put a rope around his neck. He led the horse to the fence, got on his back and here they came galloping around the pasture to where I was.

I remember thinking, "Boy, this is going to be just great riding a horse!" Weldon stopped him next to the gate and I got on.

EARLY CHILDHOOD

"Hold on to me," Weldon said and off we went. Now, sitting on a sway back horse is not the best riding place in the world.

We shot everything from crooks to Indians with our stick guns. We'd pull them from our pockets and shoot the fence post pretending they were crooks. I don't know how long we rode that poor old horse, but you could tell he was getting tired of us on his back.

There was one tree in the whole pasture—a persimmon tree. If you have eaten ripe persimmons, you know they are good. If they are green there is nothing more horrible tasting in the world. Weldon decided that we would ride old Tobey down to the tree and get us some persimmons. He got Tobey turned in the right direction and we began to shout and holler. Tobey didn't seem to like the hollering we were doing so he began to trot. The more Weldon tried to stop him, the faster he trotted, until he came to a sudden stop throwing Weldon off onto the ground. He then began to go around the pasture at a trot with me on his back. I'll take that back; I wasn't on his back. I had my leg round his neck and I was hanging on for dear life. I grabbed hold of his mane and with my feet around his neck I wasn't going any where. I thought I wasn't, but suddenly Tobey stopped.

His head went down and I went sliding down his neck and onto the ground. I landed on my back with the wind knocked out of me. I finally got up the nerve to open my eyes and did I get a surprise. Not six inches above my head was the face of Tobey looking me straight in the eyes. His lips were rolled back and if I didn't know better, I would say he was laughing at me. Horses don't laugh at people or do they? I will always believe he was laughing at me.

I slid along trying to get out from under his horrible breath and ugly mouth. I moved, he moved with me. I kept pushing myself along with my feet. I would think he was gone only to open my eyes and find him still there. He never made any attempt to hurt me in any way. It was as if he were playing with me.

I finally had all I could take and, getting to my feet, started to run toward the gate. Old Tobey ran along behind me not trying to catch up, but close enough I could feel his breath. I made the gate and went over it as fast as I could. Tobey stood there and rolled back his mouth and let out a whinny that made me stop and look back.

I had forgotten Weldon in my haste to get away from Tobey. I ran along the fence looking for him and finally saw him lying on the ground. I thought he was dead but then I could see he was moving. I hollered at him and he stood up very slowly. He started to the gate shaking his head. Old Tobey saw him up and started toward him. I yelled for Weldon to watch out. Weldon ignored Tobey and climbed over the gate. With the both of us on the safe side of the fence, I walked over to Tobey and stuck out my tongue. I got the surprise of my life for he let out a whinny that sounded like a laugh. I watched as he trotted back across the pasture.

I know that horses don't laugh at people nor do I believe that they play with you. That wild ride was this old boy's first and final ride. I had no desire to go chasing bad guys on horseback after that. There had to be a better way. I decided that it would be better to give chase to the bad guys behind the wheel of a car. I did my chasing of the bad guys in the luxury of an automobile as a police officer!

White Flower

There are all kinds of memories carried around in the minds of people. Wouldn't it be enjoyable if they all were good! I have an unforgettable memory of my third grade school teacher. It all started when I began school in the first grade. My teacher, Miss Susie, would talk to me but I wouldn't answer. I grew up with my family calling me Burt. But at school my teacher called me Lonie, so I didn't answer. One day she carried me home to tell my mother that I had a hearing problem, only to find out that I didn't answer to Lonie. After that, when she addressed me, she would say "Lonie Burt" and I'd answer.

When I entered the third grade, I had Miss Susie again as a teacher. I liked her and was glad to have her again for another year. I remember a time when all the kids were to bring a flower to school for their teacher. I went home that day wondering where I was going to get a flower. We had none at home and I didn't have any money to buy one. This was upsetting to me. That evening I began a search for a flower. I went though the neighborhood but no one had a flower to give me. That night when I went to bed my father came in to see that we said our prayers. I remember praying for a flower for Miss Susie.

I got up the next morning and started to school. Still no flower. I went down the switch track to where I met the other boys and girls on the way to school. They all carried flowers. I was the only one who didn't have a flower. I walked along behind them feeling out of place. They were laughing, leaving me out of their conversation. We got to Hill Street and as usual, we started to cut across the vacant lot at the corner of Elm and Shorter. The closer I got to the school, the slower I walked. I had my head turned looking down at the ground.

A friend of my said, "come on Lonie. You're going to be late."

I looked up to see who had spoken to me and my eyes could not believe what I saw in the bushes.

There, standing above the bushes, was a white flower! It was a white flower to me but now I know that it was a type of weed that has what looks like a bloom. I went to it, breaking it off and ran to catch up with the others. I wanted them to see my flower. They began to snicker when I showed it to them. Someone in the crowd called it an old weed. No one can be as cruel to a kid as another kid. Nothing could have hurt me any more than having my flower called an old weed. I walked slowly behind the others and was the last to go into the schoolhouse. As I came though the door, I remember someone saying, "Here comes Lonie Burt the weed boy."

I dropped my head and got into the end of the line.

The line formed out in the hall and as you went though the door, you handed the teacher her flower. Everyone was looking back at me and sniggering. I remember looking down at the floor trying not to pay attention to what was said.

There was this one girl who was a little snob. She came running back to where I was and stuck her flower in my face. "This," she proclaimed, "is a flower! What you have is a nasty old weed!"

I didn't say anything, just kept looking down at the floor.

She ran back to the front of the line saying, "weed, weed, nasty old weed!"

My time came and ,still looking at the floor, I offered my flower to Miss Susie. She placed her hand under my chin and raised my head. She said, "Thank you. It is a beautiful flower and I appreciate it!" She took the flower from my hand and began to trim the stem.

I walked to my desk and sat down, watching as she placed the flower in the middle of the others. The white looked to be snow white among all the other colors. I knew that everyone was looking at me as I smiled and sat up straight in my seat.

If there was ever an angel then Miss Susie Davis, my teacher at Elm Street School, was one.

The Broken Gun

Christmas had come and gone and as usual the traditional orange, apple and stick of peppermint candy were received. It was hard for a small boy to understand how come Santa Claus brought all the other kids wagons, bicycles and all kinds of toys. It seemed that by the time Santa got to my house, he had run out of toys and only had fruit and sticks of candy left! I would sit in the window and watch the kids play with their toys in the street. I knew if I went outside they would want to know where my toys were. Since I didn't have any, it was much better to stay inside until the new wore off of their toys. It didn't take long for most of them to tear up what they had received for Christmas. But my brothers and sisters and I learned to be thankful for what we did get and not to question it.

Well, one year a bit after Christmas had come and gone, something happened that I remember to this day. There was a grocery store on the corner of Shorter and Division that was called the Home Store. It was run by a man by the name of Burton. My mother would give me a note of what she wanted and fold the money in it and tell me to give it to Mister Burton. He would gather up the items and I would take them back to her. This trip to the Home Store was like so many others I had gone on before. I walked the railroad tracks to Division and then went up to the store. Past the railroad were houses on both sides of Division Street. The West Town Plaza shopping center is now located there.

There weren't many cars on the road back in those days. You

had to walk in the road since sidewalks were nonexistent. I was walking along and I could not believe my eyes for there in the middle of the road was a gun! I ran over and picked it up. A piece of the barrel fell off. I picked it up, got out of the road, and marveled at what I had found. There on the handle was a picture of Red Ryder. I held it and looked at it as if it were gold. I had never had a toy pistol to play with! Up until that time, I had used a stick and now to have a real Red Ryder pistol was something unbelievable.

It never occurred to me that it belonged to anyone, because after all, it was thrown away and left in the road. I went on to the store and gave Mister Burton the list and waited until he filled the order and placed it in a sack. He had watched me play with the broken cap pistol and laughed saying, "be careful and don't shoot yourself in the foot!" We both got a laugh out of that and I headed back home.

I could hardly wait to show my gun to my Mother. I never realized that she would do what she did.

She took one look at it and said, "Young man, where did you get that gun?"

"I found it in the middle of the road," I replied.

She put up the groceries and then said, "Take me and show me where you got that gun."

"I found it," I said again.

"You know that you don't pick up any thing that doesn't belong to you."

That was one thing that we were taught: never pick up anything that didn't belong to us. I had broken the rule and brought a gun home that didn't belong to me. Try telling a small boy who had never had a cap pistol to play with that he couldn't pick up a broken gun lying in the road. I remember thinking that I had done a really serious thing. It was back up the railroad with my mother to the house on Division Street where I had found the gun. We went up to the door and my mother knocked.

I remembered that I stood frozen, holding the gun in my hand. I watched as the door opened and a lady came out. My mother explained what we were doing and told me to hand the gun to the lady.

She smiled at me and took the gun. "Yes," she said, "that belongs

EARLY CHILDHOOD

to my son but he got mad and threw it in the road. I never went out to get it and he didn't either. Your son did not steal the gun for it was laying broken in the road."

My mother and the lady talked for a few more minutes. As we started to leave, the lady called out, "wait!" She went back into the house and came out holding a belt with two holsters. In one of the holsters was a gun that looked new. She stuck the broken gun in the holster with the other one and said, "Raise up your arms."

I didn't know what she wanted but raised my arms. She bent over and fastened the belt around me. I looked down and saw one of the most beautiful sights. Two holsters and two guns around my waist! She gave me one of the most beautiful smiles I had ever seen. "They are your guns now."

I looked at my mother to see if it was okay to take them. She smiled and nodded her head.

"Thank you!" I said.

"You're welcome. My boy didn't play with them anymore, so you take them and enjoy them."

On the way back home I know I must have strutted wearing those two Red Ryder guns and holsters.

left to right:
Benny Abernathy,
Billy Joe Byrd,
Lonie with his guns

I tried to fix the barrel on the broken gun but couldn't. I took a rubber band and tried to fix it, but the broken piece kept falling off. I was on the back porch when a man who lived in the area came by. This fellow had talked to me a lot after my father passed away and I had learned to like him. His name was Ben.

"What you got there?" he asked.

I showed him the broken barrel and how I had wrapped a rubber band around it.

He looked at it and said, "Let me have it and I'll fix it for you."

I gave him the gun and he left, saying, "Give me a couple of days."

The next couple of days passed slowly while I waited on my gun. A few days later we were at supper when someone knocked on the kitchen door. I went to see who it was. There with the gun in his hand was Ben! The gun looked so new you could hardly tell where it had been broken. I gave him my best smile and said, "Thank you!"

He handed me a small box. "Here are some bullets for your guns." It was a pack of caps. I thanked him again and he left. I wore those guns for many years and was proud of them.

From that experience, I learned not to pick up anything that didn't belong to me. I also learned there are some good people in this world who are willing to help you. Ben was one of those people for he helped a small boy when he needed a friend the most. The lady who gave me the guns saw a small boy who would take them and enjoy playing with them. I have fond memories of people who were good to a poor small boy when I was growing up.

House on the Hill

When I was a small boy growing up in West Rome a friend and I would do what we called sack fishing. A creek ran through an area known as Coligni, from West Rome parallel with John Davenport Drive under a bridge and to the river. The new post office now sits in that area. Where the Church of Christ now sits there was a big house. My friend and I would slip into the woods below the house to sack fish and pick up hickory nuts. The woods were full of what we called scaly bark hickory trees.

The Big House

My friend and I were caught several times by the lady who lived in the big house. She'd take half of our hickory nuts away from us. That was, as she put it, the price we would have to pay for slipping in and picking up her hickory nuts. We would stand and look at the big house on the hill and watch the people as they moved about. I had no idea that some day I would see the insides of that big house.

A lot of years passed. It wasn't until it after I had married that I got to see the insides of that house. My in-laws, Clyde and Addie Worley, lived in a house that was behind the big house. They looked after the place because at the time no one lived in the big house. The family had all passed away except for two women who lived uptown. I was there on several occasions when they would come out and check on things at the big house. Addie introduced me to one of the women and it was she who showed me though the big house. All the old furniture was still in it at that time. It looked the same as it did when it was first built. It was indeed something to see.

converted slave quarters where Lonie's in-laws lived

The house that my in-laws lived in was built as servant quarters when the big house was built. My wife and I would go up on Sundays and spend time with her parents. I would laugh at Clyde when he told me that the house they lived in was haunted. Addie would back him up. I had a good laugh at some of the things they would say happened. For instance, they both insisted that a woman in white would walk though the house at night. Clyde said that once he went into the kitchen to get a drink of water. He was standing with the water in his hand when a woman dressed in white walked by him. I smiled at that.

He said, "I'm telling you the truth. I know you don't believer it, but it happened."

The woman in white I never saw but something else happened that made me think.

It happened on a Sunday. Addie had cooked one of those old fashioned dinners, one that had chicken with all the trimmings. While the women were in the kitchen fixing the dinner, Clyde was showing me a new 28 gauge shotgun he had bought. Clyde and I went rabbit hunting back in those days. He handed me the gun and said, "It's not loaded."

I've handled guns most of my life and never took anyone's word as to whether a gun was loaded or not. I checked to make sure it wasn't loaded. Clyde handed me three shells. I took the shells and put them on a table that sat in the corner of the room. I looked the gun over and then placed it in the corner next to the table unloaded. We were told the food was on the table so Clyde and I went in to the dining room and sat down to eat

After the meal, Clyde and I went out on the porch and sat down. At that time we both smoked so we had a cigarette and talked, leaving the women to clean up the kitchen. It wasn't too long before Addie and my wife came out and sat on the porch with us. We sat there talking when from inside the house came what sounded like a gunshot! We all jumped up and ran inside to see what had happened. There on the floor in the middle of the living room lay the gun that I had placed in the corner. Lying beside the gun was a spent shell. I stood there, not believing what I was looking at. I looked at the table where I had put the shells. Two of the shells lay there but the third one was gone. I reached down and picked up the gun and the shell. I put the spent shell on the table and turned the gun toward the wall. I then gave the gun a thorough check to make sure that there were no shells in it. I looked at Clyde.

He shook his head and said, "I told you that this house was haunted!"

Clyde and Addie have passed away and gone is the big house and the servant quarters that were behind it. My wife and I often talk about the time that the gun went off leaving a hole in the ceiling. I have never found an explanation for what happened. Clyde believed that it was a ghost that fired the gun. Did a ghost fire that gun? I don't think so. I do know that the gun was unloaded and the shells were lying on the table. This remains one of life's mysteries.

Barber Shop

I remember my first barber shop haircut. Most of the time when we were growing up, a person in the neighborhood cut the kids' hair. You came away with what was called the bowl cut. All of the kids who went to the lady who cut mine came away with bangs. I got to the point to where I didn't want a bowl hair cut and decided that there had to be something I could do. I knew a barber shop haircut took money. Money was something that I didn't have.

A neighbor who lived close to us had a man who would come and split wood for him. One day I was close by and heard them get into an argument. The argument grew heated and the man who was splitting the wood walked off. He yelled, "I quit! Get someone else to do your dirty work!"

I watched as my neighbor started to split the wood. It was easy to see that he had never split wood before. I watched as he turned red in the face and threw the ax down.

"Mister Wells," I said, "what do you pay to get your wood split?"
He turned and looked at me. "Kinda little for this, aren't you?"
"I'm big enough, sir," I replied.
"Yes, I guess you are." He smiled. "See those two racks? This one is stove wood. Fill it full and I will give you a dollar. This one is for fire wood. Fill it and I'll give you a dollar and half. Fill both of them today and I will pay you in the morning."

The rest of the day was no fun, but before I quit that evening, I had both racks full. I went home and told my mother what I had done.

The next morning I went to collect my money. Mr. Wells met

me at the door and handed me the money. I took it, feeling like a rich man. He smiled as he watched me fold the money and stick it in the bib of my overalls.

"Fill those racks every Friday and you will get a payday every week," he told me.

"Yes sir!" I said and started home to show my mother all the money I had.

When she saw it, she said, "It's yours. You spend it for what you want."

I worked and saved my money for the next three weeks. I then went to town and straight to the barber shop that was in the Cotton Block. I remember there was only one seat empty.

The barber said, "Right back here, young man."

I crawled up into the seat.

He said, 'See those pictures on the wall? While I get you ready, look them over and show me the hair cut you want."

I pointed to one of the pictures and he smiled, saying, "One haircut coming up!" He cut my hair and then put some oil on it, combed it and then turned me to where I could see in a mirror.

"Well?" he asked. "What do you think?"

I could not believe what I was seeing! That couldn't be me. I paid him and walked out on the street a different person. I then went up the street to a five and dime where I bought shoes, pants and shirts. I even bought a new shiny belt to hold up my new pants.

Monday morning when I joined the other kids walking to school, they all looked at me but didn't say anything. As I entered my classroom and sat down, Miss Smith, my teacher, looked at me sort of funny. She stood up and said, "Class, would you welcome the new student."

We all looked around. I didn't see any new student. She walked over to me and put her hand on my shoulder. I realized she was talking about me! I looked up and said, "I'm not a new student! I am Lonie!"

She smiled down at me and said, "A nice looking Lonie. There are boys in this class who could learn a lesson from you."

The rest of the day no one said a thing about my shoes, shirt or pants. It was all about my barber shop haircut.

Last Dance

We moved from West Rome to Fourth Ward. Where the Western Sizzlin' is now was a field with one house sitting in it. This was called the short end of West Ninth. When you turned off of what is now Turner McCall Boulevard onto Martha Berry Boulevard, which was a two lane road at that time, on your left there was a church. A row of houses sat on a street that ran in the same direction as Martha Berry now runs. As I remember, people called this the short end of Avenue D. There were three or four houses on it. To get to the house we lived in by car, you had to come up Desoto Avenue and turn where the AAA Transmission shop is now located.

It didn't take long for me to make friends with a boy who lived on the short end of Avenue D. His name was Jimmy. Jimmy and I were friends for many years until he passed away. We would go to what was called the Projects where there was a play ground. Those houses are now being torn down and as they go, so go some good memories. On Saturday nights the play ground would be full of kids.

One night, Jimmy told me of something that was hard to believe. He said he could show me where we could go dancing. I knew that neither Jimmy nor I could dance but it sounded like fun. I was game, so I said, "Let's go dancing." Try, if you can, to imagine two bare-footed boys about the age of ten going dancing. Now picture one of them wearing overalls and a bowl hair cut: me!

I will always remember that Saturday night when we slipped away from the rest of the kids. Across North Fifth where the high rise is now located was a row of houses. As you continued toward town, there was a vacant lot. As best my memory serves me, there was one building along that stretch of sidewalk. It later was known as the P.S. Cleaners, I believe. Sitting in the field was a building that had at one time or another been a warehouse. This building had big double doors on the North Fifth Avenue side.

I followed Jimmy down the bank beside the building that later become the cleaners. We took up a position behind a concrete column that had been under another building at one time. People were arriving, some in cars and some walking. Just at dark, they shoved the two big doors open. This gave us a good view inside the building. It didn't take long before the music started. I watched wide-eyed in disbelief. That night gave us something to talk about all the next week. I promised Jimmy come Saturday night I would go dancing with him again.

In the weeks to come we were there dancing as we called it. One particular Saturday I will never forget. It started as usual with us taking our place behind the concrete column. It was a hot night so it wasn't long before the doors were slid open. We sat there taking it all in. Jimmy would stand up and do a fancy dance step and I would laugh at him.

Then from inside someone let out a scream and people began to pour though the door. Then we heard "Bang! Bang!" and someone yelled, "Call the cops!" People were running, crouching down behind cars and anything that offered protection.

Jimmy and I lay down behind the concrete column as close to the ground as we could get. Then a couple more gun shots came from inside and a man came to the door and shot in the air. We could hear sirens coming in the distance. A police car slid in and two policemen jumped out of the car, drawing their guns.

Someone yelled to the policemen, "Watch out! He's drunk and got a gun."

At that time a second police car came sliding into the lot. The first policemen had taken up a position on both sides of the door. The other two joined them and they all burst though the door at the same time. It got quiet, with no sound coming from inside. Then two of the cops came out bringing a man with them. They placed him in the back of the patrol car and left.

Then the other two came out and one of them said, "All right, all of you people hit the road." He took out a flashlight and shined it around the lot. "You!" he yelled shining the light in our direction. "If you're still here when I come back, you'll go to jail!"

I got my feet under me and left in a hurry! As I crossed the playground I remembered I had left Jimmy back there. Then I saw someone running off the other end of the playground. It was Jimmy. He stopped and waited for me. We didn't talk, we just moved faster getting home.

Later we talked about going dancing again some Saturday night, but that was the last dance that we ever went to, as far as I know. If you mentioned dancing, a chill would go up my back and the words of that big policeman would come back to me: If you are here when I come back, you will go to jail!

Jingle Money

In the early forties money was hard to come by. And you know the old saying "if you are willing and able, good things will come your way." Back then if a young boy got any money, he would get it in change. He'd put the money in his pocket and walk around listening to it jingle. This was called jingle money. The boys liked to hear it jingle in their pockets.

There weren't too many ways for a young boy to make money. My way was going around gathering up bottles. I had a small red wagon and after school I would get out and look for bottles. Soda bottles would get you a penny a piece. Milk bottles were worth a nickel a piece. Whiskey bottles would bring a nickel a piece from our local bootlegger. I could get a penny a piece for the home brew bottles from our friend in the neighborhood. He made home brew and sold it to all the locals who drank. He would keep the brew on ice and there were always people coming and going from his house. This was especially so during the summer.

On the corner of what was called Scant's Corner back then was a field. This field was where the old health department is located. This field was grown up to where you couldn't see into it. The locals would carry their brew and whiskey to the field and drink. People in the neighborhood knew what was going on in the field but no one cared as long as the drinkers stayed out of sight.

Any time I went in the field, I would find a bunch of bottles. The fellows got to know me and soon they would hide the bottles so only I could find them. The other boys would look in the field but would have no luck. I would always come away with bottles and they couldn't understand it. That was my secret I had with the locals who drank.

One week I was lucky. I found a bunch of milk bottles. I went to the field when I was sure no one was watching me. I went to where the bottles were hidden and loaded them in my wagon. I started to pull on my wagon but the wheel had gotten stuck on something and I couldn't move it. I went behind the wagon and pushed but it still wouldn't move. I picked up the back of the wagon and shoved. The wheel came loose bringing a piece of wood with it. I moved the wagon off the wood and was fixing to leave when I saw them. There in a hole covered by the board was a stack of whiskey bottles. I picked up one and removed the top. The smell was awful! I poured the awful smelling stuff out of all the bottles and put them in my wagon. All the way home I kept thinking how lucky I was to find the whiskey bottles.

I washed my bottles and placed them in a box that I kept for hauling them to the store. I counted up how much money I would get when I sold them. I had seventy five cents worth of bottles! I couldn't believe it. It had been the finding of the whiskey bottles that had given me so much money. At that time I didn't realize that what I had found was where old Jake the bootlegger hid his whiskey. I thought that it was just some bottles that someone had put there. I didn't realize that I was pouring out old Jake's whiskey. I also remember that what was in the bottles was the worst smelling stuff I had ever smelled.

Early the next morning I loaded up my bottles and started out to sell them. My first stop was old Jake's place. There was a street that ran off West Tenth and made a circle back onto what is Martha Berry now. Old Jake lived in the first house coming in from the Martha Berry side. He looked at my bottles kind of funny and asked, "Where did you get them, son?"

"I found them out there in the field," I answered.

He reached in his pocket and counted out the money for the bottles.

"Thank you, Mister Jake!" I said, heading for West Tenth with the home brew bottles.

If I had known then what I know now, I would have never sold Jake any bottles. With the home brew bottles sold, I started to Jackson Fruit Stand which was on the corner of West Ninth and Martha Berry. I sold my soda bottles to Jackson Fruit Stand and then started to the dairy. The dairy was on Shorter Avenue just below where Shorter Heights Florist is located. The road was all uphill but after quite an effort I made it to the dairy. Heading back toward home was easy for it was all downhill. I got home, went in and put my money on the table to count. I could hardly believe it, for this was the most money I had ever had! Seventy-five cents in all. It was all in jingly money.

I put my money in my pocket and went out to play marbles with a group of boys. I got in the marble game and began to lose, so I decided I would stay out of the game and jingle my money. I watched for a while, but then decided to get back in the game. I was bent over shooting marbles when I heard, "Adcock, I want that jingle money in your pocket."

It was Russell, the neighborhood bully. All the boys in the neighborhood were afraid of him. I have always thought that being afraid and being a coward are two different things. I have been afraid many times, but have never been a coward.

I straightened up and backed away from him. Several men in the neighborhood had stopped to watch us boys play marbles. They sat down under a tree and were talking. When Russell yelled "I want that jingle money," they stopped talking and started to watch us. I backed up, reached down and picked up what I thought was a rock. Russell ran at me trying to get ahold of me. I sidestepped him and let go with the rock. What I had thought was a rock was a clump of dirt. The clump hit him between the eyes and came apart, filling his face and eyes with dirt. There must have been a small rock in the dirt because there was a small cut on his forehead. He wiped away the dirt. When Russell looked at his hand and saw blood on it, he let out a scream like he was dying and started to run. I watched as he crossed Martha Berry and headed down West Ninth still screaming. I saw him as he went into his house.

I didn't know what was going to happen so I turned back to playing marbles.

"Here he comes!" one of the boys said.

I looked up and saw Russell and his father coming up West Ninth toward us. I looked around and saw what we called a sand rock. I picked it up and put it in my back pocket.

Now what I saw would have been funny if I hadn't been scared. Russell's father was a big fat man. He was as big around as he was tall. He was almost in a run coming up West Ninth. He reached the group of us boys, face red and out of breath. It took him a few minutes to get enough breath to speak. Then he bellowed, "Who hit my boy in the head with a rock?"

"I did, sir," I said.

He looked at me. I took a step back only to realize someone was standing behind me. I looked up into the face of one of the men who had been sitting under the tree. He was the one they called Harper. I can't recall his last name.

"Why did you hit my boy with a rock?" Russell's father asked.

"He tried to take my jingle money, sir," I replied.

"He what?" asked Russell's father, his face turning red.

I drew back and put my hand in my back pocket.

The man called Harper said, "The boy is telling you the truth."

Russell's father looked down at Russell and said, "You've lied to me not once, but twice today." He grabbed Russell by the seat of the pants and they headed back down West Ninth.

I looked up at Harper and said, "Thank you sir, for helping me."

"Just remember," Harper said, "take up for yourself."

I headed home feeling like a winner. I found out later that Russell's father dusted off the seat of his breeches real good, the old fashioned way. I had lost all of my marbles but I was still a winner. In the early forties there weren't many boys my age that had a pocket full of jingle money. I felt good walking home with my hand jingling my money. I do not recommend what I did to Russell as a way of taking care of a bully. I will say it quieted him down though, and I don't ever recall any of the boys having any more trouble out of him.

Valentine

There are certain things that happen early in life that you wonder about for years to come. Once such incident happened to me when I was in the seventh grade going to Neely school at the foot of the city Clock Tower. I am sure there are still people around who went to the old Neely school. I remember the climb up the hill which was especially tough during the winter months. If there was ice on the ground it was a job getting up that hill. Going down was much faster! I remember walking between the sidewalk and the curb in order to get up the hill.

When I went there, Neely held the sixth and the seventh grades. I had gone though the sixth grade with most of the other children and knew them. On Valentine's Day we gave out valentines to the other kids. There was always a special girl that you would try to get the prettiest one for. As the valentines were being given out, you would watch and try to catch the expression on the special girl's face when she got it. When you received that special card, you would see that look as she looked at you. If she smiled, then you would smile back. If she frowned, you scooted down in your desk as far as you could.

This particular Valentine's Day was like so many others. When you came in you dropped your valentines in a box by the door. At the end of the day the teacher would put the box on her desk and call out the names on each valentine. I remember that the box was full and everyone seemed to be getting their share. I would read each one as I got it and then look around at the one who sent it. I remember the smiles coming my way and I felt like I was ahead of the rest in getting valentines. Then the teacher reached in and took out what looked like a box. She held it up where everyone could see it. It was a small box of candy with a valentine tied on it with a blue bow.

Then she said, "Lonie, this is for you."

I remember I sat there too numb to say anything.

"It's yours Lonie! Come and get it," she said, holding it out to me.

I got up and made my way to the front of the room with every eye on me. I reached out, took the box of candy, turned and looked at the faces in the room. I hurried back to my desk and sat down. I stared at the box of candy with the blue bow on it.

I finally got up enough courage to remove the blue bow and take the valentine off the box. There, written on the back of the valentine, were the words: *Lonie, I will always love you.* I shall never forget them! There was also a picture of a girl holding a heart that read, "You will always have my heart. It is yours forever."

I looked around at the faces in the room but they didn't tell me anything. I have wondered all of these years who sent me that valentine with the box of candy. The rest of the time that I was at Neely, I tried to find out who it was. No one ever came forward and admitted sending it to me. This has remained one of life's little mysteries!

Part 2

TEEN YEARS

Rabbit Hunting with a Rock

At the time of this rabbit hunting incident, I was sixteen and working for a construction firm. It had been a bad year for outside work and the weather wasn't getting any better. We had only gotten in a couple of days of work and it was the week before Christmas. It looked like Christmas that year was going to be slim. Christmas was on a Saturday. I remember it very well because I picked up my pay on a Thursday and was told to check back on Monday to see if the weather would let us work. I gave the money to my mother so she could pay the bills and get groceries with what was left. This would be another Christmas where the boys would get an orange, apple and a piece of stick candy. When I went to bed that night, it was beginning to sprinkle snow.

When I got up the next morning the ground was covered with several inches. I remember looking out the window and thinking it was Christmas Eve and we would have beans for our Christmas dinner. We would be thankful for them. Back in those days beans and potatoes were just about what people lived on, if they could get them.

Then an idea occurred to me. I put on my warm clothing and headed outside. I told my mother I was going rabbit hunting.

I remember she laughed. "What are you going to do? Run them down and catch them?"

By this time in my life, I had had lots of practice pitching baseballs. One of my early childhood friends was a baseball addict. He could play pitch for hours and got me interested. At a young age

I developed my arm to where I could pretty well put the ball where I wanted it. We moved from West Rome to Fourth Ward and there I met another friend who liked to pitch ball. His name was Charles and we would pitch for hours. I kept training the arm and it got better and better with age. By the time this rabbit hunting incident took place, I could go squirrel and rabbit hunting with rocks as my only weapon.

So, on this Christmas Eve, I went walking down to the railroad tracks to a field where the Rome High School now sits. There were no roads in that area at the time. When I got to the railroad, I started to size up some rocks to hunt with. I heard a voice call my name. I looked down the tracks and saw a boy who lived in the neighborhood. His name was Carlton and he had a shotgun.

"Where you going?" he asked as he watched me pick up and feel the rocks.

When I found a suitable rock, I put it in my pocket. Having found several for my pockets and one for each hand I started down the railroad with him. He showed me the new 410 shotgun that his parents had given him for Christmas. I remember thinking it was a beauty and wishing I had one. He told me they had let him have it a couple of days before Christmas so he could go hunting in the snow. We came to the field and he headed out toward the middle of it.

If you have ever hunted, you know that there are hunters and then there are *hunters*. There are people who know what they are doing and those who don't. Carlton was one of the latter. He got to the middle of the field and yelled, "Run rabbits! Run for your life for Carlton intends to have rabbit for supper!"

I stopped and let him get out in front of me.

He let out a yell. "There he goes!" and emptied his gun at a rabbit. He reloaded his gun and started to run after the rabbit.

I stood still with my rock, waiting. Now as anyone who has been rabbit hunting knows, if you stand still that rabbit will come back to where he jumped up from. I watched as Carlton stomped around the field hunting for the rabbit.

In a few minutes, the rabbit came hopping back. I let fly with one of my rocks. Number one was in my sack. I walked on down to where Carlton stood waiting for me. It wasn't long before 'bang,' 'bang' and 'bang.' Carlton missed again.

I waited, standing still, and soon here came number two for my sack. I started toward home waving to Carlton as I left. He never knew that I had two rabbits in my sack for Christmas dinner. As I was leaving the railroad tracks heading up to my house I heard 'bang!' 'Bang' and 'bang' again!

Christmas was spent inside for it was rough weather outside. The table was set and I sat down along with my two small brothers. A platter of fried rabbit was placed in the middle of the table. On one side of the rabbit was a bowl of gravy and on the other was put a big bowl of mashed potatoes. On each end of the table was a plate of biscuits cooked in a wood stove. I know that there are not too many people living nowadays who have eaten a piece of fried rabbit with mashed potatoes and a biscuit covered in gravy. On that day we had a Christmas dinner fit for a king.

I don't think Carlton ever got him a rabbit for his supper.

Back when times were hard, people hunted small animals for food. I did back then but now I put out food for them in the winter. I couldn't hurt any kind of animal now.

Ghost

I remember an incident I call my experience with the paranormal. This happened in 1944. My friend Jimmy and I were going to a party on Pennington Avenue. Back in those days there were two ways of getting places: walking or riding the bus. Since money was hard to come by, walking was the way most of us got around.

Jimmy and I had just gotten to the South Rome bridge when we heard someone yell at us. Two boys we knew were coming down the street so we waited on them.

Lonie at about the time this ghost story took place.

"Where are you going?" one of them asked.

"To a party," we answered.

Eddie laughed. "Over at Skeeter's?" he asked. Skeeter was a very large boy. How he had gotten the nickname no one knew.

"We're on our way over there also," Robert, the other one, said.

We turned down Brannan Avenue and headed across the playground. At that time the city had a playground with swings, seesaws, and other things there at the foot of Myrtle Hill. We went though the park and along a dirt road at the cemetery. Skeeter lived in the block just past Myrtle Street. We arrived in just a few minutes. Skeeter greeted us with a hot dog in one hand and a coke in the other. We jumped right on the hot dogs and then played games. In those days you didn't stay out too late. At about ten o' clock, time was called and the party broke up.

The four of us went back down Brannan Avenue. Since it was dark we stayed on Brannan Avenue instead of taking the dirt road at the foot of the cemetery. We crossed over to the other side, for we had heard people talk about the haunted house. As we approached it, someone let out a low moan. We all stopped.

Then Eddie began to laugh. "Got you that time!"

Not thinking that was funny, we all turned toward.

"Come on fellows! I was just funnin'." The rest of us didn't think it was funny, standing there in front of the empty houses.

"Look," Eddie said, "I got a quarter that says no one here will go through that house." He pointed to one with an open door.

Robert said, "I got another quarter that says no one here will go."

"Here's mine," Jimmy said. "Lonie, where's yours?"

"Don't need one," I said. "I'm going to take all the money by going through that house." I handed Jimmy my quarter anyway. "In case I don't make it."

With Jimmy holding the money, I headed for the steps to the porch. Turning, I waved and stepped through the open door.

If I live to be a hundred, I will never forget the feeling that came over me. A chill went up my back and it felt like I had stepped into an ice box. I walked into the room which was dark except for a little light that came from a street light outside. I moved further into the room and stopped in front of a fireplace. I was not too sure of what I saw or heard from that moment until I jumped off the back porch. As best as I can recall there seemed to be smoke in one corner of the room. There appeared to be a mist of some sort in the middle of the smoke. The smoke was dark with a white mist in it. The white mist seemed to separate from the dark smoke and start toward me. I froze. I stared at it as it seemed to drift closer. There seemed to be a face in the white mist. The eyes were piercing. I felt a chill cover my whole body.

I was frozen stiff! Then I heard someone call my name. "Lonie! Are you all right?" It was Jimmy calling me from the front porch. I moved, running through the house and onto the back porch. I never stopped for the steps; I just jumped off the porch. I stood for a moment, still trembling from the cold. I remember I didn't want the other boys to think I was scared, so I calmly walked to the front where they were. They watched as I approached wide-eyed. I remember one asking, "What was you doing standing there in the middle of the room pointing?"

I didn't recall that I had been pointing while I was standing by the fireplace. I started to walk toward South Broad trying to get warm, for I was still cold.

This time, as I recall, it was Eddie who asked, "What were you pointing at? We could see you from the road."

Jimmy handed me the money. I held it and said, "it's yours if you'll go back in the house and see what I was pointing at!"

We walked across the bridge with very little conservation among us. Robert and Eddie went out Second Avenue. Jimmy and I went up Broad Street. We stopped at Krystal so I could get a cup of coffee because I was still cold. Jimmy left me at Fifth Avenue. I crossed over and sat down on a bench to wait for a bus. Where the parking deck on Broad and Fifth is today was a Sears store at that time. I drank the coffee and a little warmth returned to my body.

As I look back and try to recall the events that took place inside of that house, they aren't clear to me. The one thing that is clear and that I will always remember is on a hot, muggy July night, I almost froze to death. When I think about it after all these years, I still get a chill up my back.

Ghost Hill

I was living in North Rome on Reece Street in the 1940s and was working with a construction company building all kind of buildings. One Friday I was asked to come in and work a few hours on Saturday. Working Saturday meant overtime but it also interfered with my weekend. The overtime won out so I went in. We took longer than I thought and didn't get off until around two o'clock. I went home, took a bath, and was sitting on the porch waiting for supper when a friend of mine, Duke, who lived up the street, came down.

He sat down and asked, "What are we going to do tonight?"

I was tired but didn't intend to stay home on a Saturday night. I shook my head and said, "Nothing. Just cruise around."

Duke owned a Hudson automobile. This was one of those cars that you could put six people in. There were two seats that pulled out of the back of the front seat. These were for small children.

Duke grew quiet and I could tell he had something on his mind.

"You got some thing to do tonight?" I asked.

"Well yes, in a funny sort of way," he said.

"What do you call a funny sort of way?" I asked.

"You know Frances who comes to the park?"

There was a park at the corner of Reece Street and Callahan at that time. There were young kids and older boys and girls there most of the time, most of whom I knew.

"Yes, I know Frances and most of the rest," I answered.

"Well, Frances and some of the other girls want us to take them to what she calls Ghost Hill."

That set me back as I remember, for I had never heard of Ghost Hill. "Where is Ghost Hill?"

"I'm not sure, but somewhere down around the Narrows on the Alabama road."

I thought for a minute remembering my earlier encounter with a haunted house, then said, "Sure why not? I haven't seen any ghosts in quite a while!"

Duke got up to leave. "I'll round up the girls and wait for you."

I watched him as he was going up the street wondering what I had let myself in for.

Much later, Duke pulled up and blew his car horn. To my amazement he had a car load of girls! They were crammed in like a can of sardines. They made room for me in the back seat and I crawled in, surrounded by girls. Duke had to go all the way to the lower end of Reece Street to turn around. As we started back up the street, I asked, "Where is this Ghost Hill?"

Frances started to tell us about Ghost Hill. She said it was out Highway 100 between the Alabama Road and Summerville. Now at that time Highway 100 was a small road full of pot holes.

According to Frances, the Indians over in Alabama had a running battle with the white man. The Indians eluded the white man and crossed into Georgia. Thinking they were safe, they camped on a small hill. The white men had followed them, however, and while the Indians were asleep, killed them all men, women and children. I have never verified whether the story was true or not. I remember at that time I got a chill listening to Frances tell about going down there and hearing the moans and groans. Everyone in the car had gotten quiet and I remember thinking that this was the first time I had ever heard this group that quiet!

Dolores, a very small girl, was sitting beside me and I could feel her trying to scoot closer to me. I smiled. This was going to be fun! In those days there was nothing I enjoyed more that scaring someone. Mean, never. Mischievous, always. We drove around until it got dark, then headed for Ghost Hill.

It was a warm summer night and the moon was bright. We came to Ghost Hill which wasn't much more that a rise above the side of the road. As we went up the dirt road which ran to the top of the hill, it began to get steeper, then came to a flat top. There was a spot where there was nothing growing and you could tell where cars had been. Duke turned the car around to face the road.

Now Frances said, "Everyone roll down the windows." Since it was summertime and cars didn't come with air Conditioning, the windows were already down. Everyone sat quietly, listening for the groans and moans. Suddenly I got a funny feeling on the back of my neck and started to turn and look at the back glass. Delores let out a scream and jumped out of the back seat against the front seat. I turned and looked at the rear glass. My face was inches from it. I remember jumping, grabbing the door handle and opening the door. I still think that I saw a face looking though that glass at me! I came out of that car faster than I had ever exited a car before! I ran around to the back of the car. No one was there. I looked around the car but saw nothing.

When I jumped from the car, Duke had gotten out with a safety tool in his hand. We moved away from the car and looked in the brush that was growing around the area. Nothing was in sight. The moon had the night lit up almost as bright as daylight.

"You got a flashlight?" I asked.

He brought me a flashlight and I bent down and shined it under the car making sure no one had hidden there. Nothing. I was standing by the car door while the other girls were trying to calm Delores down. I heard something behind me, turned and saw nothing. But there seemed to be someone making noises in the bushes around us. I knew that no one was there because the bushes were blackberries; no one could walk around in them.

Frances came around the car to where Duke and I were. "Do you now know why they call this Ghost Hill?"

"I haven't seen anything to make me believe that a ghost is here," I said. I have often wished that I had not said that! A rustle of the bushes and a weird sound came from a tree that stood on the edge of the clearing.

"I got you now!" I exclaimed, going over to the tree. I thought someone was hiding in the tree. I shined the light in the tree but saw nothing. I was getting tired of chasing nothing and got back in the car.

We sat there for a few more minutes. Then noises that sounded like moans and groans floated out of the darkness. Duke and I agreed that we had enough of Ghost Hill for one night. We left hightailing it out of there with little Delores sitting so close to me you could hardly see her.

After a long discussion we decided to go over to Roy's Drive-In and get something to eat and listen to the talk of the town for a while. I listened to the others and got their opinion of what had happened. Delores swore she saw a face in the glass behind us. I didn't say anything. I knew I heard some moans and groans. Others heard talking and people walking. One girl—I can't remember who—said there was someone with me when I went checking out the tree. I knew I had a feeling that I wasn't alone but didn't see anyone. Again the question: do I believe in ghosts? I know that there are some things you can't explain and some things you leave alone.

After Duke and I had let the girls out that night, we drove around doing some more talking about what happened. We both were in agreement that we would not go back to Ghost Hill and bother those spirits if they stayed away from us! As far as I can remember, I never went back and bothered them and they have never bothered me.

Drink The Punch

Recently, I was thinking about an incident that took place in the late 40s. I was about sixteen or seventeen and lived in North Rome on the lower end of Reece Street. At the corner of Callahan and Reece was a park that was a hangout for the boys and girls in the area. One Friday evening we were all in the park when a girl who lived on North Avenue walked over to me and a boy name Carlton and invited us to her birthday party. I had been to a party at her house before. There had been as much cake and other goodies as we could eat.

"Do we have to dress up?" Carlton asked.

"Wear what you want to," she said.

Carlton replied, "I always wear my overall pants." What are called jeans today were called overall pants back then. Most boys bought them too long and turned up a cuff in the bottom.

"We'll be there," we told her as she was leaving.

"I'm going home," I told Carlton. "Come by the house and I'll go with you."

Carlton came by the house just as it was getting dark. We crossed the railroad and went up to her house through the back yard. I mingled with the crowd for a while and then noticed a big bowl of punch sitting on a table on the porch. I got me a glass and filled it. Just as I was starting to taste it, Carlton came over and grabbed my arm. I looked at him thinking, *what in the world is the matter with you?*

He pointed to the bowl of punch and whispered, "Don't drink it!"

"What's the matter with you?" I asked, pulling my arm away.

He motioned for me to follow him to the end of the porch where no one was.

"Carlton," I said, "if you don't tell me what's the matter, I am going to pour this punch on you."

He looked around making sure no one could hear him. "It's the punch! Hal poured a pint of white whiskey in it!"

I shook my head. "You're kidding!"

"No, it's the truth."

I poured my punch over the porch rail and on the ground. Walking back to the punch bowl, I got the surprise of my life. The bowl was empty! Everyone there had a glass and was drinking it down. You are probably thinking that there wasn't enough whiskey in the punch to matter. Well, take a bunch of teenagers who never drink anything stronger than coffee and put alcohol in them and see what happens.

I sat down on the porch railing and watched the alcohol take effect. There was an unusual amount of loud talk and laughter. I noticed some were lying on the grass in the front yard while others were lying on the porch. I got a piece of cake from the table and backed up against the wall by the door. Then I heard a loud moan and the punch spiked with alcohol came up. I knew that this was no longer a place for me, so on my way out, I picked up as much of the cake as I could carry and headed up the street. I had turned the corner at the light when I hard someone call my name. I stopped and looked back. Carlton was running to catch up with me.

"What happened?" he asked.

"I thought you said that there wasn't enough alcohol in that punch to hurt anyone," I said.

"Hal said he put a pint in it."

I knew that a pint of whiskey wouldn't have caused that much damage to the kids. I had my hands full of cake, so when we got to the railroad we stopped at a cafe that was located there, went in, ordered a coke and ate the cake. The evening that had promised to be fun had turned into a disaster.

I didn't think much about what had happened after we left, but later I found out. A group of us was sitting around in the park when

Hal came over. He started to laugh and told us how he had put a quart of white whiskey in the punch bowl. A quart, not a pint, had gone in the punch. It was a wonder that some of the kids hadn't wound up in the hospital. I let Hal know that I didn't think it was funny.

He stood up and in a loud voice exclaimed, "You don't like it?"

I started to walk off. He ran over and grabbed me by the shoulder. That was the wrong thing to do because my elbow to his stomach put him on the ground.

Standing over him I asked, "Where did you get the quart of whiskey that you poured in the punch?"

He sat up and whimpered, "I stole it from a bootlegger on Chamber Street."

"I think I'll go over and tell him that you stole his whiskey."

"No! You can't do that! He will kill me for stealing his whiskey!"

I sat back down on the bench and Hal got up and sat beside me.

"You know you got a lot of kids in trouble when you poured that whiskey in the punch. Go over and tell the lady who gave the party what happened so she can tell the mothers of the kids who got in trouble with their parents." I stood up again, ready to leave.

"Will you go with me?" Hal begged.

"No," I answered, "you go and if you don't, I'll go tell her what happened *and* I will tell the bootlegger that you stole his whiskey."

The other kids had been standing quietly by, not saying anything. When I walked away, they went with me leaving Hal alone. He looked like a scared puppy who didn't know what to do.

I found out later in the week that Hal did go over and tell the lady what had happened. The kids who drank the punch and got tipsy were let off the hook.

That incident taught me to always smell what I was drinking if I didn't know what was in it. And I will always remember that a quart of whiskey in a punch bowl made a lot of innocent kids sick and got them in trouble with their parents.

Part 3

---◆---

ARMY DAYS

Lady Liberty

The best way to pull up memories is to go through old pictures. One day I was scanning pictures into my computer and as I pulled them from the album, memories just seemed to jump out at me. There were quite a few of in my Army uniform. Of course my Army memories started with a letter from the President:

> *Greetings from the President of the United States. You have been selected by your friends and neighbors to serve in the Armed Forces of the United States of America . . .*

I was sent to Atlanta on Halloween, 1950. There I was examined and told to get all of my business in order, for I had passed and would be inducted into the Armed Forces in a few days. Sure enough, a few days later, the letter came instructing me to report to the Draft Board which was in the West building on East Second Avenue. Bright and early, I was put on a bus loaded with young men and sent to Fort Jackson, South Carolina. A period of processing began in which we were read the Articles of War. It was my understanding that you couldn't be sworn in until the Articles were read to you. I was given a series of tests to determine what outfit I would be placed in, which turned out to be a Signal Construction Unit, the 315th Signal Construction Battalion, to be exact. I stayed at Fort Jackson for training.

After Basic Training, and then some special training, we were given a few days leave. When we arrived back at camp, we were told that we would be shipped overseas. A mark up of our equipment said we were going to Korea. A few days passed and we were still at Fort Jackson. We were given a three-day pass and told to be ready to move out when we got back. But after our three-day pass was up, we were still sitting around Fort Jackson doing nothing. Nobody seemed to know what had happened. We were taken back to our equipment and told to change the marking. We did and were told we were on standby alert and to be ready to move.

Lonie at the beginning of his Army days

Then we did move. We were placed on a train and sent to Camp Kilmer, New Jersey. Our time for the next few days was spent in briefing and taking shots. We were told that we could get a pass to go to New York. Transportation would be furnished to those who wanted to go. Did I want to go? A herd of elephants couldn't have stopped me! That night everyone was excited about seeing the sights of New York, but I never dreamed it would be anything like it was. (This was back in the fifties, not like it is today.)

The next morning bright and early found us on a bus headed for New York. I was seated on the single seat behind the driver, so I had the best view. I watched as we approached a long bridge that crossed a river between New York and New Jersey. I must have had my mouth open as I stared down at the river.

The bus driver chuckled. "I cross this bridge at least twice a day and the scenery never ceases to amaze me. I grew up in Jersey and have driven a bus for the Army for the past twenty years. I make this trip at least once every day."

He stopped talking as the traffic began to move, so I sat back and took in the sights. There were large ships and small boats all over the water.

The bus driver spoke again. "In a few hours when the town comes to life, the river will be as full of traffic as the roads are."

I remember thinking, *what a sight that must be!*

We drove off the bridge and into nothing but tall buildings. The going was slow because the streets were full of traffic. Finally the bus driver pulled into what appeared to be a train station. He parked and stood up.

"Listen up, you fellows," he said. "These buses will be here until 12 o'clock midnight. At exactly twelve, we'll pull out and head back to base. You must be here no later than twelve. One last thing to remember is that no one gets lost in New York who has cab fare." He opened the door. "You're on your own until then."

We began to unload and look around. I looked for my buddy Robert, who came over to me and asked, "Where to?"

I looked around and shook my head. I had no idea where I was so it didn't matter which way we went. I remembered what the bus driver had said. "If you got cab fare you cannot get lost in New York." So we hailed a cab and Robert told him to take us to the Empire State Building. The cab driver smiled and then pulled into the traffic at a high rate of speed as if he were in a hurry. I soon learned that all the cab drivers there drove as if the were going to a fire.

At the Empire State Building, Robert and I got out of the cab. I looked up and there, swaying in the sky, was a building so tall I couldn't see to the top of it.

"Come on!" Robert said opening the door and heading inside. I followed slowly. I had no desire to go into a building that tall!

"Come on," Robert urged as he headed for the elevator.

The elevator door opened and he stepped inside with several other people who were waiting. I stepped inside too and heard a chuckle. A lady sat on a stool operating the elevator. She smiled at me when I hesitated getting on. The door shut and we started upward. I knew I had made a mistake for my stomach begin to feel funny. I looked over at the woman who ran the elevator.

"Want off?" she asked. And

I nodded my head yes. The elevator came to a stop and the doors opened. I stepped out.

"Wait here," she said. "I'll be back to get you in a few minutes."

I saw a bench and walked over to sit down. A little bit later, I saw the light over the doors of the elevator come on indicating it was stopping. The doors opened and I stepped in.

The operator smiled. "Don't like elevators?" she asked.

The door closed and the bottom of the elevator fell from under me. I grabbed a rail and held on for dear life. It couldn't have taken more than a second before the floor flew up and hit me. The doors opened and I stepped out of the elevator and looked back at the operator. She gave me a smile that said 'sorry about that!' I found a bench and sat down. It wasn't too long before the elevator doors opened again and Robert came out. He had a grin on his face as he looked at me.

We must have ridden in ten cabs that day. When we thought of something we wanted to see, we'd jump in one and away we would go. We went to the park where they had a small carnival and watched people ice skate. Time was passing, and we started to look for something to eat.

"I know!" Robert said as he waved down a cab.

As we got in the driver asked, "Where to, fellows?"

Robert said, "Anywhere we can get a big steak with all the trimmings."

"Know just the place," the driver answered as he gunned it into the traffic.

I wasn't sure but it seemed to me that we were going around and around the block before he pulled in and stopped.

"Here you are, fellows! The best steak in town."

I stepped out, looking around. There on a window I saw 'Jack Dempsey Cafe.' Robert was staring at the window with an odd look on his face.

He shook his head and said, "Not *the* Jack Dempsey?"

I opened the door to the café and was not prepared for what

greeted us. There, painted on the wall, were pictures of Jack Dempsey and the people he had fought in the ring.

I was studying the paintings turned when a voice said, "This way, please." A waitress led us to a table.

I was still amazed at the pictures as we sat down. With our orders taken, the waiter left us. Robert and I talked as we looked at the pictures on the wall. As we talked, the people around us began to get up and move closer to us. A strange look came over Robert as we became surrounded.

"Fight or run?" he asked.

I turned around so I could face the people.

A voice from behind me said, "No reason to be alarmed, fellows. They mean you no harm."

I turned to see who had spoken and looked into the face of the big man himself.

I must have looked surprised, because he said, "Welcome! I'm Jack Dempsey and this is my cafe. These people have been listening to you talk and wanted to move in close to where they can hear you. They've never met anyone from the South. We don't see too many Southerners here in New York! So relax and enjoy your meal."

An elderly man got up and came over to our table. "We are so sorry! We didn't mean to alarm you." He then invited us over to his table.

Robert and I were happy to move over to their table. The others moved in close to us and we had an enjoyable conversation until our food came. We stayed for awhile after we were finished eating, but finally had to say we still had some more of New York to see. When we went to pay our bill, the cashier just smiled and pointed to the other side of the room where Jack Dempsey stood.

"Your bill has been taken care of by the man himself," she explained.

We waved our thanks and stepped outside.

Robert shook his head. "No one will ever believe us when we tell them we met Jack Dempsey!"

Truer words were never spoken. Whenever I have mentioned this story, I can see the disbelief in people's eyes.

Just then, a cab pulled up and we hopped in. It was the same driver who had brought us here to Jack's cafe.

"Where to?" he asked.

"Times Square!" we told him.

We took off again on another ride of our lives into traffic. Before we could blink he was stopping. We got out in the middle of Times Square and began to walk and look around. It was indeed amazing just to walk and look at everything. One can only imagine what it looks like today. We came to Rockefeller Center where a long line of people was standing. There we saw that a special show was being put on by the Rockettes. We started to walk off when a lady standing in line spoke to us. I turned to see what she had said. I remember that she said, "Yes, I'm talking to you, soldier boys." She asked, "Are you stationed around here or on your way overseas?"

"On our way overseas," I replied. "We're just here for today."

She held out two tickets. "Take our tickets and see the show," she offered.

I shook my head. "We couldn't take your tickets."

"We live here and can see the show another time."

"Take them," urged the man who was with her.

I reached out and took the tickets. "Let us pay you for them," I said.

"No," the lady replied. "They're our gift to you in appreciation for your service to our country."

I will always remember the couple who gave us the tickets even though I never knew their names. Then the theatre door opened and they began to move us inside and usher us to our seats. It took time to get all the people in and seated in the huge theatre. Music started to play and what followed was something to see. How long that show lasted I don't know, but it was amazing!

When it was over and the lights came on, Robert and I sat until the last of the people filed by on their way out. It had gotten dark so we decided to go back to where the bus was parked. As we got in the cab I told Robert that this would be our last ride in one. The cab dropped us off at the bus. We were hungry again, so decided to look for a place to eat.

We discovered a place where you could walk though and see sandwiches and other types of food inside a little glass door. The price of each item was on the front of the glass. A lady sat at a counter where you could get change. After finding what we wanted, we sat down to eat.

One of the fellows who rode into the city with us came over and sat down. "Where have you been? We're all at the bus ready to go!"

It had been quite a day. The river at night was something to see. It was lit up like a Christmas tree. My bunk sure felt good that night!

Early the next morning we were loaded into trucks and taken back to New York this time to board ship and head out. We were loaded aboard a ferry and carried to Staten Island. After an Army band played *Dixie*, we went aboard ship. I will always remember gazing at Lady Liberty standing proud holding her torch. I remember thinking how beautiful she was. As beautiful as she was that day, the next time I saw her she was even more beautiful.

USNS GENERAL Wm. O Darby

Christmas Away From Home

I knew that this Christmas would not be the same for it would be the first one away from home. I was stationed in Germany, far away from my family gathered around the table eating and enjoying themselves. Since money was hard to come by, material things were something other people had. But we had love of family. A closer family than ours didn't exist. I remember lying in my bunk in the Army barracks looking up at the ceiling and wondering what my family was doing this Christmas. I remember going to sleep with that on my mind.

The next day was Christmas Eve so we didn't have any duty to pull. We had donated some money to buy toys for some kids in an orphanage and after dinner we were going over to present them with toys. At the orphanage, my fellow soldiers and I gathered in a small room and lined up around the wall. We were each given a package with a name on it. I remember the name on my package as if it were yesterday. The name was Greata. I could tell that the package contained a doll.

We waited until the kids were brought into the room and lined up facing us. A lady who spoke English gave a talk about the orphanage. She told how long they had been in operation. The children in the room with us were only a few of the children in the orphanage. The others were at a similar event elsewhere.

I looked at the small children on the other side of the room standing quietly. I noticed that they wore name tags so I begin to look for the one who was Greata. There in front of the rest stood a small girl who looked as if she was scared to death.

Oh great, I remember thinking, *they gave me the one who is scared of everybody*. The lady who was doing all of the talking finally ran down and we were told to find the child whose name matched the one on our gift had our name plate and give them the present. The other fellows had no problem giving their presents for I could hear the tearing of paper. I approached the little girl whose name tag read "Greata" and extended the toy to her. A look of pure terror came into her eyes. She backed up and hid behind a little boy who was shooting everybody with a cap pistol. I turned and looked at the lady who had given the talk.

She came over to me and I said, "She won't take it."

"Come sit down," she said, leading me to some chairs. I sat down while she went over to the little girl and picked her up. She hugged her and said something that I couldn't hear. The lady brought the little girl over and put her down in front of me.

"Please take off your cap," she requested.

I removed my cap and watched the little girl's face.

"Now," she said, "offer her the toy."

I extended the package toward Greata. At first she drew back. Then I gave her one of my biggest and warmest smiles. It worked! Greata reached out and took the package from me. Just as she touched the package, a smile came across her face. That made my day. I watched as she tore the paper from the doll. Then, as little girls all over the world had done before, she took it in her arms and hugged it.

We loaded on the bus and got back in time for supper. After supper I went to the command conference room to see if I had received any mail. There on the table sat a big box, a small package and some letters for me. I picked up my mail and carried it to my bunk. I then went to the PX for the rest of the evening. Again, I went to sleep thinking of Christmas with the family.

The next morning after breakfast I went back to my bunk and opened up the box. I couldn't believe my eyes! The person had sent a cake and it was broken into small pieces. I left the cake on my foot locker for the fellows to enjoy. I t didn't last long even if it was in small pieces.

It was a long day even with Christmas dinner with all the

trimmings. I could see my family gathered around the table with my spot empty. I was the person missing but I had hopes that by next Christmas I would be back home. There is nothing as bad as that first Christmas away from home. Just ask any veteran.

Roller Skating

I've been trying to recall the first time I went roller skating. As I recall the first time I ever had on a pair of skates was with my friend Duggan. He pulled up in front of my house with some others in a car. I was sitting on the porch.

"Come on," he said. "Let's go skating."

"Go where?" I asked, wanting to be sure that I had heard him right.

"Roller skating," he repeated.

"Where are we going skating?" I asked.

"We're going up to Pennville."

I had never been on a pair of skates in my life, but I got in the car with them. When we arrived, the others couldn't wait to get their skates on and get on the floor. I held back waiting for them to start.

Duggan came over to me and said, "Get a pair of skates and come on."

So I paid my fifty cents, got me a pair and put them on. I tried to stand up and found that it wasn't as easy as the people on the floor made it look. Stumbling and grabbing on to everything I could, I made it to the floor. I watched the others for a few minutes then hit the floor. When I say hit the floor, that is exactly what I did. I hit the floor by dusting off the seat of my pants! I remember getting up and looking around to see anyone saw. They did; I could see the smiles on their faces.

I was determined to skate even if it broke my neck. I moved out on the floor in a position that today seems impossible to get in. I headed straight for the jukebox which sat in the corner of the room. I grabbed onto it; it was me and the juke box. We did a sort of dance with me holding onto the juke box and taking it out on the floor. The rest is history.

Houston 'Duggan' Farmer

I became addicted to roller skating from that day forward. I went skating quite a few times with Duggan. One time I went with another friend to Chattanooga to a skating rink that was on Market Street. My friend had moved from Chattanooga to Rome, so he was familiar with the area. When he found out that I liked to skate, he told me that he had a sister who worked part time at a skating ring there. I don't think that I have ever seen anyone who could skate like her. I talked her into giving me some pointers on what to do. Skating is not something that you can do without practice. Practice is what I got that summer and if I have to be the one to toot my horn, I'll say I got quite good at it. I think we went everywhere there was a skating rink that summer. The one that I liked best was the one in Chattanooga. It was converted from an empty store that had gone out of business. It was huge. After one circle, you had to stop and catch your breath.

ARMY DAYS

Life was good that summer until Uncle Sam decide to write me a letter. You know the letter I am talking about. The one that began with "Greetings from the President of the United States of America." After much training and a short time later I found myself in Germany. At that time most of the country was under construction from the war. I found myself in a place where there wasn't much to do that fitted my lifestyle. When free time came up, the others went uptown. I tried that but found very little of interest. I visited places of interest but found myself back at the barracks when it got dark. The other soldiers found refuge in the local guest houses, night clubs or beer gardens as they were called by the soldiers. Being a non-drinker, I had very little interest in those places.

It was on a Saturday evening after supper that I went to the PX to see if any of the fellows were there. I got myself a coke and sat down. There was no one in the PX so I played a couple of record on the jukebox. I was standing by the jukebox when a WAC came in. I watched as she bought an item from the girl at the counter. She was leaving when she saw me.

She came over to where I was. "What's the matter, soldier? Are you lost?"

"Something like that," I replied.

"Why don't you 315th boys ever come down to the roller rink?" she asked.

Did I hear her right? Did she say roller rink? I remember asking, "Where would there be a roller rink at this place?"

"Follow me," she said. "I'll show you where there is one."

I followed her and she pointed out a building that I had seen before, but didn't know what it was. I followed her though the door and into what looked like heaven away from home to me. A huge skating rink and a snack bar! There were people sitting at tables in the snack bar and the floor was full of skaters. The WAC motioned for me to come with her. She led me over to where a woman was behind a half door with a counter built on it.

"She'll take care of you." The gal left me there and headed over to a table full of people. I was handed a card to fill out and once that was done, given a number. Whenever I came in and wanted a pair of skates, I would give the woman at the counter the number and she would give me a pair of skates. With the skates on I hit the floor doing a little fancy step or two as I went. I remember thinking how good it felt to be on a pair of skates again. It didn't take long for me to make some new friends.

Most of my free time was spent there at the skating rink. I had some good times with my newfound friends. I remember one WAC called Midge. Midge weighed somewhere around 200 pounds and stood a good six feet tall. The 200 pounds was muscle, not fat. She was a mechanic at the motor pool for the WAC detachment.

Anyone who has ever skated has played Train at one time or another. Train is where you line up behind each other and hold on to the person in front of you. I've seen a line of skaters that circles the entire floor. One of the nights when the floor was full, a game of Train got started. The train grew until there must have been at least twenty five people in it.

Midge was the caboose and as she came by, I grabbed on. I became the caboose and it took me a while to get around the rink. I believe it was on the third swing that someone broke the chain and fell in front of Midge. Midge's feet went out in front of her and she fell backward. Midge had a soft fall for I was there to cushion it. The trouble was there was no one for me to fall on! I remember trying not to fall where she would land on me. She landed on top of me anyway and my head slammed the floor. The lights went out. I came to lying on one of the couches in the lounge. A soldier was working on me. I found out later that he was a Medic from the 12th Armory outfit. I tried to sit up but he put his hand on my shoulder.

"Easy," he said. "You all had a nasty fall."

I almost laughed out loud at the way he said *you all*. I learned later he was from Macon, Georgia. An ambulance attendant came in and they hustled me off to a medical building on the base. After a while they decided that I was all right and carried me back to the rink.

I got a kick out of a nurse when she saw the skates on my feet. "You boys from the South wear skates instead of shoes?" she asked.

I remember replying, "Only when we get tired of walking!"

I went back to the skating rink with orders that if I had any kind of headache or other problems I would report back to the medical building. All the others were waiting for me. I can truly say that I have never been hugged as much as I was that night. And Midge, she very gently hugged me with tears rolling down her cheeks.

"It's okay," I remember telling her. "I'm still here and kicking."

I didn't kick very much or very high for the next few days. I didn't quit skating until years later. The last time I was skating was at Turkey Mountain with a school group. That was many years ago but I still have good memories of when I could skate with the best.

Peter

When we arrived in Germany we were stationed for a few months in a town called Pirmasens. Pirmasens was headquarters for the Signal Corps. This town was in the mountains where the snow got several feet deep during the winter. We arrived in November and the snow and ice were waiting for us. After Pirmasens, we moved to a town called Worms in the Rhine River Valley. Moving from the mountains to the valley was like leaving Rome and going to Key West Florida in the middle of January. The weather was cold, yet pleasant. I saw very little snow while stationed in Worms. We got our fill of snow while on maneuvers in the mountains.

Our motor pool was several blocks from our barracks. During the walks over, I didn't pay much attention to the children who were outside the gate. I began to notice that they seemed to be there only at certain times of the day during the week. On the weekend the children hung around most of the day. As the soldiers walked to the Motor Pool the children would follow them. The soldiers were always good for a chocolate bar or some other type of goody.

There was this one boy who stood back and didn't approach the soldiers when they came out the gate. He would look at every one of them then go sit down. I decided to see if he would take a candy bar from me. That first morning I offered him a candy bar, but he refused it. I tried for several weeks before he accepted it. He got to where he would come over to me and follow me to the motor pool.

I asked, "Do you understand English?"

He nodded his head yes.

"What's your name?"

In perfect English he replied, "Peter."

That was the beginning of my friendship with the little German boy named Peter. Peter wasn't very talkative at first. He would walk along beside me not saying a word. I kept trying until I got him talking. I had what was called a class A pass, which meant that any time I didn't have duty, I was free to go anywhere off the post I wanted to. On Sunday evenings after dinner I would go the park on the Rhine River and just relax. The river had all kinds of boats on it, so I would just sit and watch. I got to be friends with an old German who would come down to the river to fish. He spoke a little English and I understood a little German so we could communicate.

One evening I was sitting on a bench watching the old man fish when someone sat down on the bench with me. I turned and was surprised to see Peter sitting there.

Lonie in Worms, Germany, with German children.
Peter is behind Lonie, waving.

He gave me one of his sad smiles and said, "You like it here?"

"Yes," I remember replying, "it's quiet and peaceful here." I looked at the little boy sitting there and asked, "Peter, how old are you?"

"I am ten," he said and grew quiet.

We sat there for a while before I told him I had to get back to the barracks.

As he was leaving he asked, "Do you come here very often?"

"Every Sunday if possible," I said.

I spent quite a few hours on that bench talking to that little boy. The one thing I have never forgotten is his sad smile. You could look at him and he would be smiling but his eyes were sad. I wondered why he would look at the face of each soldier as they came though the gate.

I got the answer before I was shipped out of Germany back to the States. I had come though the gate one Sunday morning going to the park and was surprised to see Peter standing there. He was very seldom at the gate on Sunday. I spoke and he came over to me. He called me by my name which he seldom did.

"Lonie," he said, "my Mother wishes you come to our house today."

I was taken aback for he had never mentioned his parents. I agreed and we started for his house. I had no idea, where he lived but followed him. He began to tell me that his mother worked at an American club for servicemen. He had never talked as much as he did that day on the way to his house. It wasn't far to his house and we got there in just a few minutes. I was familiar with the area because of the service club for the soldiers. He opened the door and I followed him inside. There stood a woman whom I had seen at a skating rink run by the Armed Forces. She worked in the snack bar. She seemed to be as surprised to see me as I to see that she was Peter's mother.

I learned that day why Peter had such a sad smile. I also learned why he looked at each soldier's face as he came though the gate. On a small table was a picture of a soldier which she said was Peter's father. Peter's mother spoke both English and German. She had taught Peter English with the hope he would get to America one day. I learned that Peter's father had shipped back to the States and she had not heard from him. She waited, hoping that he would come back and get her and Peter and bring them to America. I was told that he had been gone for over a year and they had not heard from him. I left there that day understanding why the smile on the little boy's face was sad. Now I also knew the reason that he watched the faces of the soldiers at the gate.

His heart was sad even when he gave you the big smile of a ten year old. Day after day he stood searching for the face of his father among the soldiers who came though the gate. I was there for almost a year after meeting Peter's mother and his father still had not came back. The last thing I remember about Worms, Germany was a little boy sitting by the gate looking at faces of soldiers. I was on the back of a truck leaving when I saw for the last time the little boy called Peter.

Part 4

Police work

POLICE WORK

A special Thank You to all the fine police I served with over the years

I joined the Rome Police Department when most of the old policemen were nearing retirement. We had Chief Smith Horton and Assistant Chief Horace Stewart. Those gentlemen are no longer with us. I recall that you would likely find Cecil Stewart, C. H. Peck, and Horace Collins directing traffic on Broad Street. They were regulars on the day shift. A few more of the old group were Bill Kinney, Bill Tierce, Darrell Brumbelow, Joe Cook, George Lemming, David Jones, Gus Horne, Bob Ware, Gene Pope, Willard Nelson, Howard Long, Frank Perry, Chandler Phillips, Don Unsworth, Paul Poston, Thomas Sims, Leonard Bolt, O. W. Pierce, Jack Dye, Paul Reynolds, Lester Blaylock, R. D Brock, J. B. Hankins, Sonny Adams, Milt McConell, and Archie Lawrence. Red Bradshaw rode a three wheel motorcycle on Broad Street. John Barnett, Hoyt Owens, D. G. McCoy, Gene Freeman, and Joe Cleveland were also motorcycle cops. And last but not least, my first partner in a patrol car, Wallace Wilson, known to us all as The Whizz.

At that time, we had three captains—Captain Jess Freeman, Captain Red Couch, and Captain Nelson Camp. There were two detectives, Oscar Williams and Bell Terhune. There were just two patrol cars for the entire city, one on duty from seven a.m. to three p.m., and both were on duty from 3 p.m. to 7 a.m.

As the old guard slowly changed, young officers came on the force. I remember Paul Rampley, Troy Autry, Troy Young, Randy Garrett, Pete Pilcher, Doug Williams, Harper McDaniel, Randy Michaels, John Pledger, Don Vick, Danny Crabbe, Ralph Kilgo, Tom King, Elaine Snow, Theresa Kitson, Deniese Downing,

Pam Richey, Stephen Hill, Mike Reynolds, Mike Ragland, Lonzo Roberson, Travis Goss, Terry Autry, Stephanie Hill, Mary Smith, Terry Murchinson, Gary Clayton, Ann Stewart, Vern Pitts, Bobby Pearson, Carla Pearson, Kenneth Kines, David Burkhalter, Randall Murphy, Pat Cleveland, J. W. Scott, Lamar Clark, John Walters, Ralph Bishop, John Smith, Wayne Atchley, Doug Meers, Bill Harris, Mike Jones, James Soloman, William Hibberts, Larry Treglawn, Freddy Stewart, Archie Duvall, Larry Pope, James Milan, Stuart Honea, Charles Weaver, Roy Duvall, Brad Blalock, Buzz Salmon, Tommy Pruitt, Hubert Smith, Bill Bohannon, Roy Talent, Floyd Phillips, Danny Jackson, Tom Bojo, Mike Thornton, Stan Banther, Wayne Craft, Marshall Smith, Jerry Penney, Doug Tolbert, Greg Brock, and Lavone Ward.

The radio operators were Robert Byars, Betty Minshew, Carol Whaley, Virginia Floyd, Emma Hammondtree, Jean Crump, Mark Blanton, Donna Harris, Jody Lumpkin, John Kohler, Norma West, Daniel Smith, Johnny Burchfield, C. C. Satin, Linda Dew, Greg Chambless and Mary Mosteller..

Working records were Lorraine Sutton, Debbie Marshall, Ann Briley and Glenda Gordon.

During my career as a police officer, I worked under seven chiefs: Smith Horton, Ted Peacock, Nelson Camp, Frank Perry, Billy Hart, John Collins and Joe Cleveland.

I'm sure I have missed mentioning someone. Please put it down to lack of memory, and not a deliberate oversight! That happens as you get older. I worked with so many good people over the years and watched the police department grow from two cars and foot patrols on Broad Street to the much larger force it is today. I'll never forget my time with The Whizz. He taught me so much about how to be a policeman as we rode together all those years ago.

I appreciate being part of the lives of so many good people. To those who have gone on, God Bless. To those who are there now protecting us, may God protect them and guide them through this life.

Christmas in the City

All the Christmas lights and decorations were up and music was drifting from every store. The bells were ringing on every corner filling Broad Street with holiday cheer. Small children walked from store to store with their parents. The looks on their faces as they were approached by the big bearded man in a red suit were priceless. Parents were looking for gifts, and trying to hide goodies from the children. Kids urged moms to hurry up, laughing excitedly.

This particular memory of walking the Christmas beat is one of my fondest. That day was cold. It had been raining most of the day and the wind blew hard coming down Broad Street. Every now and then a speck of snow would float by. But the nasty weather didn't stop the bells ringing loud and clear from the kettle people.

I stepped into the street lowering my head to keep the wind from blowing off my cap. Once in the street I started to walk the yellow line down the center. Traffic was blocked up across Second Avenue to the South Rome bridge. The officer on the Second and Broad beat was standing in the middle of the street tooting his whistle and directing traffic. Nothing moved however, so I walked on down toward him to see if I could help.

As I approached the intersection, he pointed toward the bridge on Second Avenue. I headed off in the direction he indicated. This is some mess, I remember thinking. Here it is Christmas Eve, not a good time for this. People caught up in the traffic began to blow their horns, which didn't help matters. I wasn't worried about the horn blowing because no one was going anywhere until I could find the reason for the jam and get the traffic moving again.

As I arrived at the center of the bridge, a police car topped the levee from the back side. I could see which car was causing the traffic jam, so I headed toward it at the same time the other officer started that way.

A frantic young man was outside the car yelling, "My wife is having a baby!"

The other officer asked, "Is there a towel or a blanket in the car?"

"No!" The young man yanked off his coat and shirt. "Here, take my shirt."

He thrust the shirt at me and I passed it to the other officer. I could see as he wrapped a small baby in the shirt. I wish I could remember the name of that officer who helped bring a bundle of joy into the world that Christmas Eve.

It had begun to mist rain and turned colder.

"What am I going to do?" asked the young father.

"Help me get your wife into the patrol car," the officer said. "Then I will take them both to the hospital." Once he had everyone settled in the patrol car, he drove straight to Floyd Medical Center.

The hardest part of the entire problem was getting the frantic father in his car and headed in the right direction. Finally, traffic began to move again.

I walked the yellow line back to Broad Street and my beat. The rest of the evening was a typical Christmas Eve on Broad Street: bells ringing; policemen whistling, horns honking, and one cold, tired policeman blowing his whistle and motioning with his hands to move the cars along.

Cisco

One day recently while sitting at my desk, I knocked some old movies off a shelf behind me. As I picked them up, I came across one that jogged my memory of something that happened quite a few years ago. On the cover of one of the movie cases was the face of a man wearing a huge sombrero and dressed in Spanish clothes. A spotted pony stood beside him. On his face was a smile that I will never forget. The smile was on the face of a man who could stand among a group of men and be a head taller than all of them. And the name of the movie was *The Cisco Kid*.

When I came out of the Army I drifted from job to job trying to find one that I liked. I found what I was looking for on the city of Rome Police Department. I really enjoyed the time I spent walking the Broad Street beat. It gave me a chance to move around and get acquainted with people. One person in particular I came to know was a boy in a wheelchair and the two ladies who looked after him. His name was Eddy and I'm sure that there are still some people who remember him.

Eddy couldn't speak but he could make a noise that let you know when he was happy. I would see the three of them coming down the street and would cross over just so I could talk to Eddy. I always had time to stop and talk to Eddy.

One day we cops were told to stay in the street because of a parade. I was standing between Fourth and Fifth Avenue about where the crosswalk is now. I had my back to the sidewalk when I heard a noise. The two ladies and Eddy were on the sidewalk. Eddy was making a noise so I would hear him. I went over and began to talk to him. I watched his face light up as I talked. The sound of drums alerted me that the parade had begun. I explained to the ladies that we were having a parade and for them to move Eddy closer to the street where he could get a good view as the parade passed. With Eddy in place I moved to the middle of the street.

The high school band came through the light at Fifth Avenue. Eddy was having himself a time watching them. Then a shout went up from the people and I turned to see what they were shouting at. There behind the band was a man on a horse. He rode tall and proud. He waved at the people and he would have the horse do a few fancy steps. I turned and looked at Eddy. He was jumping so hard that the two ladies had to hold on to the chair. The band passed by Eddy and then the man on the horse passed by. I watched Eddy as the horse got even with him. He was shouting and making his noise as loud as he could. The man and horse passed by him. Then the man whirled the horse and trotted up to Eddy, dismounted and shook hands with him. I could hear him called Eddy "Little Amigo."

I had seen lots of happy people in my life but none as happy as that little boy was. There was pure joy on his face as the man spoke to him. The band moved on but the cowboy was in no hurry. He talked to Eddy for a few more minutes, then got on his horse and, touching his hat, caught up with the rest of the parade. He rode as straight and tall as this man they called The Cisco Kid.

Squeaky

In the early 1960s I was walking a beat on Broad Street. One day there were only two of us to cover Broad Street so I had been assigned the beat from the middle of the block at Third Avenue to Sixth Avenue. I was on the three-to-eleven shift. At that time most of my time was spent in the street keeping a check on traffic. Traffic was usually heavy until about six o'clock. After the traffic slowed down, I met the other officer at the old Victory Cafe which was in the middle of the block at Third Avenue and had supper.

After eating we came out on the street and talked for a while. It had gotten dark while we were inside. I started to walk out my beat to make sure everything was okay. I noticed a woman on the other side of the street motioning for me. I crossed over to where the woman stood in front of Sterchi's Furniture Store. I could see that she was very excited about something that had happened.

"Is there something that I can help you with?" I asked.

"Officer," she said, "you are not going to believe this!" She paused to catch her breath. I waited for there was no reason to rush her. She shook her head and said, "No, you won't believe me." She started to walk off.

"Lady," I asked, "how do you know whether I will believe you if you don't tell me what happened?"

"There!" She pointed up the street.

I looked up the street but didn't see anything. "What's up the street?"

"The mail box," she replied. "It talked to me when I mailed a letter."

"It done what?"

"See!" she exclaimed. "You don't believe me when I say the mail box talked to me!" She turned and started off down the street.

I watched her cross the street then turned to go check on the mailbox. I looked it over carefully. Everything seemed okay. It was getting dark so I decided to back up and watch the mailbox to see if anything else happened. Stores were closing and the owners would bring out their mail and put it in the box before going home. I waited for someone to come out and mail a letter. It wasn't long before a lady who worked in a finance office came out with letters in her hand. I moved in close to the mailbox and listened as she dropped them in. Much to my surprise, a voice came from the inside of the box! It said, "Thank you for your mail. It will be taken care of."

I thought she was going to faint but she only turned pale and looked funny. She turned to me. "Officer, did you hear that?"

I nodded and checked the box again to see if the door was locked. It was. In my opinion, no one could get inside that small space. I couldn't find where the voice had come from. I knew that the postman who gathered the mail at night would be along in a short while, so I propped up on the box and waited. Several more people came and put mail in the box and each time it would thank them.

I waited beside the box until I saw the postman coming down the street. He usually had a small cart that he pushed down the street. He was looking everywhere and appeared to be upset. He crossed the street to where I stood propped on the box.

"Officer," he asked, "do you know my boy, the one called Squeaky?"

I knew Squeaky by sight but didn't know that he was the postman's boy. Now Squeaky was a very small boy at that time. When he was full grown he was still a very small fellow.

"No, haven't seen Squeaky. What's the problem?"

"He has my keys and the one to the boxes on Broad Street is among them. I've got to start picking up the mail and get it to the post office."

He started back down Broad Street and it hit me like a ton of bricks. Squeaky was in the mailbox! I called the postman over to the side where I couldn't be heard and told him about the talking mailbox. His face changed color. He walked over to the mailbox and began to beat on the sides of it. I can only imagine what it sounded like for someone sitting inside. The door opened and Squeaky came crawling out. His father set him on his feet and said, "Stand there. Don't move!" He locked the door of the box and turned to me. "If it's okay with you, I will take care of this little fellow?"

"He's all yours," I said and watched as he led Squeaky up the street. I continued my beat, glad that the mystery of the talking mailbox had been solved. I would also bet that Squeaky had trouble sitting in a hard bottomed chair the next day!

Opossum

This incident happened in the early 1960s. I was walking on the lower part of Broad Street and Whizz patrolled the upper part. At eleven p.m., we would check all the doors on Broad, then check out the alleys. Once we got to the lower end, we would go back and, as we used to say, "put our beer joints to bed." The crowd in the Cotton Block knew who was coming at eleven and by the time I got there, they were closing up. The rest of the night was spent keeping a check on the buildings to prevent them from being broken into.

On this night Whizz and I met in front of the Krystal and went in to eat. Afterwards we walked across the street and sat down in a stairway. After a while, one of the two patrol cars on night shift pulled into the Krystal and the officers went in to eat. (At that time the only restaurant open late at night was the Krystal on Broad Street.) Whizz and I were sitting there talking when the other patrol car pulled up and one of the officers got out and went over to the first patrol car. I watched, trying to see what he was doing.

Whizz began to laugh.

"What's so funny?" I asked.

He pointed to the second patrol car which was now driving away. "They just greased the door handles on the other patrol car!"

We sat quietly and waited for the other officers to get though eating.

Whizz pointed toward the door. "There," he said. "They're coming out!"

The two officers walked over to their car. The driver reached down and opened the door. He let out a yell that brought several people out of the Krystal to see what was happening.

Whizz and I were laughing so hard tears were coming out of our eyes. I will never forget the reaction of the officers when they grabbed the door handles and got a handful of grease! They cleaned the door handles and got in the patrol car and left.

As the patrol car left the Krystal, the other patrol car came back and pulled in. The officers got out, still laughing, and went inside. Then I got an idea for payback.

"Come on," I told Whizz, "let's have some fun!"

Lately, every time I had looked in a trash bin where stores threw away cardboard boxes, there had been an opossum there. We went around behind the store at the end of the alley above the Krystal and there he was. We cornered him and put him in a box. He was a small opossum so I carried him. Whizz opened the back door and I carefully put the opossum on the back seat of the patrol car. I put the box down and we hurried back across the street and hid in the stairway.

It wasn't long before the two officers came out still laughing at the greased door handles. They checked out their door handles and, finding them clean, got into the car. We watched as they started the car and backed out.

I shook my head and said the opossum must be scared! No sooner had I said that than the patrol car came to a sudden stop. The doors flew open and both officers were running around like there was fire in the car. One of them had his gun out and the other shined his light into the car. The one shining his light began to laugh. The opossum jumped out of the car and went running back down the street. Whizz and I were laughing so hard they must have heard us. They got back in to the car and went on toward South Broad.

At the end of the shift we went into the station to check out. Everyone was standing around laughing and talking. We signed out and joined in the conversation. The guys were laughing at the greased door handles, but no one said anything about the opossum.

Whizz smiled and I knew it was coming. He started to laugh and asked, "What happened to you tonight when you jumped out of the car on Broad?"

They turned and looked at Whizz. The one named Joe said, "Darrell, I told you if we kept quiet we would find out who put the opossum in the patrol car!"

Then the rest wanted to know what had happened.

"Whizz will tell you," Joe said with a smile on his face.

So Whizz told about how the doors flew open and Darrell drew his gun. Everyone had a big laugh when Joe said Darrell pulled his gun when the opossum tried to drive the patrol car.

We all started to leave. Joe walked over to Whizz and me and said, "Remember fellows, payback is hell!"

Old Timers' Bench

There were once several benches at the corner of Broad Street and First Avenue. In the mornings a group of old men would gather there trading knives and telling tall tales. I would stop and talk to them while walking my beat. I loved their tales and didn't mind getting a joke pulled on me.

There was one old gentleman who could top all the rest telling stories. His last name was Martin and he always carried a small black satchel that looked like a doctor bag. I always called him Doctor even though the bag was used to carry his trading goods. He had a good buddy everyone called Wimpy. I can still remember two of Doc's tall tales all these years later.

One morning there were six of them sitting on the benches. As I walked closer, they grew quiet.

"Morning gentleman," I said as I approached them.

They all spoke, saying "good morning."

"Beautiful day," I said.

Nobody said anything in reply, so I knew something was up. "What's the problem, fellows?" I asked.

Wimpy replied, "Officer, could we get you to help us solve a problem that has come up?"

"Sure, if I can. Be glad to."

"Well officer, Doc here has told us something that we find hard to believe and we'd like for you to hear it. Once Doc tells his story, we want your opinion as to whether it's the truth or not. Go ahead, Doc. Tell him what you told us."

Doc started up. "Well, this happened a long time back. I was just a young fellow then. I got up one morning and decided to ride my bicycle to Chattanooga. I got there in a couple of hours and decided to ride up on Lookout Mountain. Once on top I was riding around taking in the sights when a storm came up. I had what was called a bicycle raincoat tied down on the back, so I began to put it on. Now, this was a special kind of raincoat made for bicycle riding.

It had a leather strap on the bottom of the legs so you could fasten it to your ankles. That way no water could get on you and wet your pants leg. You ran your arms into the sleeve and tied those down to keep water from getting up your arms. The front closed with snaps.

"Once I had the coat on, I started to get back on the bike when a gust of wind carried me and the bike over the side of the mountain. I was tossing and turning when, as fast as the storm had started, it stopped. I don't know how long I was in the storm before it stopped. The front of the raincoat had come unsnapped and I was floating around like a glider. I looked below me and I could see the city of Chattanooga. I'm sitting here telling you it was a sight to see.

"I knew I had to do something to get down on the ground. I was gliding in over the river and could see the bridge covered in cars. I tried moving my hands and feet and discovered I could control the way I wanted to go. I saw off to the edge of town what appeared to be a stadium of some kind. I began the task of flying in that direction. As I approached I could see it was a stadium and a rodeo was going on. I began the process of moving to the ground.

But I overshot the field and came down in one of the chutes. The fellows sitting on the side of the chute scrambled out of the way as I landed. One of them had a rope in his hand. He jumped, throwing the rope up into the air. I grabbed the rope as I hit something hard with a thump. The door flew open and what I had landed on came alive. Out of the chute and onto the field he went, the biggest bull I had ever seen! He stood still and began to paw the ground and snort. Then he began to buck like crazy! There wasn't anything that bull didn't do.

I shut my eyes and held on for dear life. It seemed I was on the back of that bull for hours before he decided that he had enough and stood still. I slid from his back to the ground and headed for the stands. A couple of fellows came to meet me and led me to where the announcer for the rodeo was.

The announcer grabbed my hand and shook it. "Man, what a ride! The best I've ever seen! You've won the top prize money!" And he handed me a check.

I looked at the check and saw it was for 25,000 dollars. The announcer called a fellow over and told him to carry me down town to the bank so I could cash the check. I had never seen so much money. I had it stuffed in every pocket. I asked the fellow to carry me to the Cadillac dealership where I paid cash for a new Cadillac. I jumped in my new car and headed back to Rome.

When I drove up in my yard all my folks came out, not believing what they were seeing. They wouldn't believe me when I told them about all that had happened to me.

Doc paused with a serious look on his face. "Officer, you now have all the facts. The decision as to whether I'm telling the truth is up to you."

I looked at the faces of the old men, knowing I'd been had.

"What do you think?" Wimpy asked.

I shook my head. "I have a question to ask, Doc, before I give you my answer."

Doc looked at me seriously. "Ask," he said.

"Doc, what color Cadillac did you buy?"

Doc smiled. "A red one," he said. "Apple red."

"Well?" Wimpy asked.

I replied, "Doc is telling the truth and nothing but the truth. You see fellows, how I know he's telling the truth is anyone with that kind of money would buy a red Cadillac."

They all looked surprised as I turned and started up the street. People must have thought that there was something the matter with me because as soon as I got out of earshot, I started to laugh. I can just imagine what it looked like: a policeman with no one around walking down the street and laughing to himself.

Another time as I walked down Broad Street and crossed Second Avenue at Enloe's Drugstore, I could see that the old timers had begun to congregate on the benches. I could see that Doc and Wimpy were already there and had the attention of all the rest. I approached from the rear. It took a few minutes for them to realize I was there. They all turned at about the same time to look at me.

"Good morning fellows," I said stepping around in front of them. "What's happening with you fellows this morning?"

Wimpy spoke up. "Officer, we were listening to Doc tell about his Florida vacation."

I knew what was coming, but I said, "What happened, Doc?"

Well, of course that got Doc started. "Last week my son came and picked up my wife and me to go to Florida on vacation. We loaded up in his van an away we went. We arrived at Daytona Beach that evening and checked into a motel. After a short rest we took a walk on the beach which gave us a terrific appetite. My wife and I met up with our son and daughter-in-law and went in search of food. I can't say what the name of the restaurant was because we picked it just from reading the menu posted in the window. We were shown to a table and our order taken. A band was playing soft music which made the meal pass quickly.

"The restaurant began to fill and the music changed from a soft to a fast pace. People began to get up on the floor and dance. I had to go to the restroom so I got up and started across the floor. The floor was crowded as I picked my way through the dancers. They were dancing so fast! I don't think I had ever seen anyone dance like that. I suddenly realized that I had forgotten my walking stick and turned to go back for it.

"Then it happened. Someone bumped me. Well, I'm here to tell you that I don't know what happened after that. One leg went one way and the other went in the opposite direction. I did a spread but kept my feet moving. I never did hit the floor. I was twisting and turning and I guess the people thought I was dancing and gave me the floor. My wife saw what was happening and ran out on the floor to grab me. She would fall backward and I would pull her up and then I would lean in the opposite direction.

"The music got faster and louder. I don't know how long we were on the floor twisting and turning before the music stopped and the people began to clap. How we stayed on our feet I will never know. Just as the music came to a stop, my wife and I regained our balance and walked back over to our table.

"A young fellow came over to our table and set a trophy down in front of us. 'This is yours. You have just won the best dancers contest!'

"I may have won a dance contest but it sure didn't help those old bones of mine. We sat there a while longer watching the people, then went up to our room for the night. I know you're not going to believe this story, but if you'll come by the house, I'll show you the trophy."

I remember watching the expression on Doc's face. It never changed. If you didn't know him, you'd believe every word he said.

"Doc," I said, "keep the trophy handy for the first chance I get, I'll come by and see it."

"Any time at all! I keep it on the mantle over the fireplace."

"I got to go," I remember saying as I started across the street. Once on the other side, I looked back and wondered how someone that age could be so full of life.

It was fun to stand and talk to those old gentlemen. If I came to work down in the dumps, a visit to the Cotton Block old timers' bench would perk me up. I believe that talking to older people has helped me keep a good outlook on life now that I am an old geezer too.

I remember the last time I saw all of the old timers on the bench in the Cotton Block. It was the last Saturday before I changed shifts on Sunday. The Shift Captain had come by and informed me he was assigning me to a patrol car. I tried to talk him out of it, but couldn't. At that time I didn't know that this would be the last time I'd ever walk a beat on Broad Street.

I was standing on the corner of Broad and Second Avenue in front of Enloe's when I saw the old timers start to fill up the bench. I waited until the bench was full then started down to chat with them. I needed something to cheer me up. Maybe Doc would have a good one this morning.

"Morning fellows," I said. "How is everyone this morning?"

"Morning, Officer," they all replied.

I talked to them a few minutes, explaining that this would be my last day walking the beat. I was changing shifts and being put in a patrol car. They all had something to say about that. One of them asked if it would do any good if they went up and talked to the chief about having me assigned to the Cotton Block. I explained that it didn't work that way. Everyone rotated shift. We talked for a few minutes more and then I started up the street toward Second Avenue. At the light I crossed back over and took up a position in front of Enloe's so I could watch the intersection.

I had shared lots of good laughs with the old bench warmers, as most people called them. A lot of tall tales were told and a few of them on me. From them, I learned to laugh with someone, not at him. Those old men had taught me to be patient and listen when someone is talking. If you interrupt you might not hear the most important part of the conversation. I also learned that growing old is a pleasure, not a death sentence. To live is to love, laugh and face each new day with a bright outlook. Gone are the old timers with their bench, but I will certainly remember their wisdom.

Fine China

Whizz and I had just started the eleven to seven shift when we got a call to see a lady on West Fourth Street. At that time there were houses where Floyd Medical Center is today. We arrived at the address and checked out. The house sat on a bank with three or four steps leading up to it. I was about halfway up the steps when a man came running from the house and jumped on top of me. I went down to the ground but managed not to fall down the steps. I had turned away just as he jumped at me so he missed hitting me enough to knock me down. He missed the two bottom steps and crashed into the patrol car. As he hit the car, Whizz was on him. I joined in and we managed to put the cuffs on him.

Another car had also responded to the call. The other officers had been to this house on several calls and so knew what this guy was like. Whizz and I had taken all the vinegar out of him by the time the other car got there. The other officers volunteered to take him to jail and book him in while we investigated to see what had happened. Whizz and I went up the steps to where an elderly man was standing on the porch.

"Come in, officers," he said, "and look at what he did to his mother's chinaware."

We followed him though the living room and into a room that housed several cabinets of fine china. The cabinets were turned over and broken china was all over the room. In the middle of the room sat a small gray-haired woman. She was crying. The man spoke to her, telling her that the police were there and they had sent Harold to jail. She never looked up. She just kept on crying.

The man explained that this was a collection of china that could not be replaced. He stated that they had been married for over fifty years and they had collected it all during that time. Whizz did most of the talking. I stood looking around at the broken glass in the room.

I stood as if in a stupor. I could not believe that anyone could do this to his mother. (As time passed, I have discovered that there are *a lot* of people who can do this to their mothers.) I walked around in the room being careful not to step on anything and break it further.

The old gentleman asked, "You boys couldn't help me stand these cabinets back up, could you?"

Whizz and I began to set the cabinets up and place them in position for him. The little old lady still sat on the floor holding a plate in her hands and crying. Every time she let out a sob it would hit me. I knew that I had to get outside for a few minutes.

Whizz saw I needed a break, so he said, "Go get the clipboard and bring it to me."

I walked outside and stopped on the front porch to get some fresh air. Then I went on to the car, got the clipboard and took it back to Whizz.

He took it and said, "Go outside. I'll take the information for a report."

I sat in the car and waited for Whizz to finish up in the house. We started for the station as soon as he got in the car.

On the way, Whizz asked, "Did you ever see anything like that?"
"Never!"

He waited a few minutes before he told me not to let it get next to me. He advised me to leave the job at the station, and don't take it home. "Don't pick it back up until you come back to work."

I took his advice and it has worked fine for me. I can't say that nothing ever bothered me again for there were a lot of things that got next to me. But from that day forward, I left the job at headquarters until I came back to work. If anyone wanted to know what happened, he would have to read it in the *Rome News*.

POLICE WORK

Wallace "The Whizz" Wilson

Return of the Bully

I've already told you about a memory concerning a certain Bully. I don't think it would be fair not to tell what eventually happened to him. When I started on the police department there were more police on Broad Street than anywhere else in town. Every day at four we had to go work traffic. Broad Street could get backed up at times if someone was not out there to keep the traffic moving. The worst intersection on the beat was at Second and Broad. I've seen traffic backed up out of sight across the south Rome bridge. East Second Avenue would be bumper to bumper as well. The bank on the corner of Second and Broad didn't do any thing to help the situation.

The day that I have in mind had not been any different. I had blown that whistle so many times all I could hear was its shrill sound. Finally, the traffic began to wind down, giving me a breather when I noticed a man in an Air Force uniform standing on the corner on the left. He waited for the light to change, started across and stepped up on what we used to call an island. The island was a slab of concrete in the middle of the street that we stood on to direct traffic. This fellow was big, not fat, just tall. He suddenly stopped and turning to me, said, "Hello Papoose!"

Hello Papoose! That threw me for I had not been called that since the third grade. I looked at him not saying a word.

"Papoose, remember me? I was that big bully you beat the heck out of with a stick."

It all came back to me with a bang. I took a step back. "Big Milt, is that really you?"

"It's me!" he replied with a smile.

"You an Air Force man?" I asked.

"You remember my dad took me out of school after the stick incident?" he asked.

I shook my head and he continued, "He sent me to New York to a boys academy for unruly kids. With that stick fresh on my mind and not wanting any more, I came to my senses. I graduated school, then collage and went in the Air Force. I now fly the fast jets and enjoy every minute of it."

We talked on for a few minutes and then he said, "I always wanted to see you again and say thanks!" He stuck out his hand. I took it and we shook hands. He smiled and said, "If you hadn't come along with your stick, I hate to think what would have become of me. Well, got to run. It's been good seeing you again." He turned to leave then turned back, smiling. "Take care, Papoose!" he said and stepped down to cross the street.

I watched as he crossed Second Avenue and went on up the street. I have memories of what he looked like as a kid and what he looked that day. He walked tall and proud and you could tell he was proud of what he had become. I watched him as he disappeared from sight. I too was proud of what he had become. The old saying "spare the rod and spoil the child" makes a lot of sense. The rod had made a spoiled child into a proud one.

Donkey Kong

In the early 1960s, I was assigned to a patrol car. I had walked a beat on Broad Street and enjoyed meeting the people who came to town and those who worked downtown. But, as the old saying goes, all good things must come to an end. So did my time of walking the beat. I was placed in a patrol car with a partner whom I still remember fondly. A better partner a fellow never had. I will call him by the nickname that he was given by his fellow officers: 'The Whizz.' Every old officer remembers 'the Whizz, fastest thing there is.'

One day Whizz and I were dispatched to Hardy Avenue to see a woman about a horse in her house. I looked at Whizz and asked, "Do you know anything about horses?"

He shook his head. "I know they are four-legged animals that some people ride."

"Well, partner," I said, "one of us will have to learn and I don't have any idea who!"

"I'm driving," Whizz replied, "so you will have to corral the horse while I take a report."

I smiled, thinking, *he beat me to it this time but I'll get him the next time.*

A group of people was on the corner at a store as we came down Myrtle onto Hardy. Several fellows pointed to the first house on the left. Whizz pulled the car in front of the house and we got out.

A woman came running out on the porch shouting, "He's out back!"

POLICE WORK

I went around back and Whizz went inside to take a report.

I stared in amazement at the culprit. He was calmly eating grass, quiet and peaceful. He stood about three feet tall and was very small in stature. What to call him? I wasn't sure for I had heard them called jackasses, donkeys and burros. Which one I was looking at, I had no idea. He had a rope around his neck which trailed behind him. He paid no attention to me as I approached. I moved close enough to grab the end of the rope. Keeping an eye on him, I began to pull on the rope and moved toward a metal post stuck in the ground. I pulled the rope around the metal post and began to draw him in. He came just as gentle as a little lamb. When I pulled him pulled up to the post, I tied him up and went to check on my partner.

Whizz was standing on the porch writing while the woman shouted loud and clear for everyone to hear. I went up the steps with a smile on my face because I could see that the Whizz had listened to the woman shouting about as long as he could.

He looked up and saw me and shook his head. "Can you quiet her down?" he asked.

I walked over to her. She shouted, "Look in my house at what that horse did!"

I looked into a hallway that led though the house. The hall had all types of curio cabinets in it. They were turned over and glass was everywhere. Some of the cabinets had glass doors that were all broken. Old style lamps were lying on the floor broken. I didn't blame the woman for shouting for if it had been me, I would have done worse than shout.

Then I got a whiff of something that didn't smell good. "Whew!" I said, backing out onto the porch. That little donkey, jackass or burro, whichever it was, had used the hallway for a place to leave its manure. It was all over the floor as if it had been neatly scattered by hand.

I waved at the Whizz saying I was going to see if anyone knew who the little animal belonged to. There were several men sitting in chairs in front of the store on the corner. I walked over to them and asked if anyone know who the animal belonged to. They all shook their heads no.

Then a small, skinny boy rode up on a bicycle and asked, "What's the matter Mister Police?"

"That!" I said. "Do you know who he belongs to?"

"Yes sir, Mister Police, he belongs to old man Herman down on Cotton street. Want me to go get him for you?"

"Yes, go tell him to come get his donkey, jackass or burro. If he doesn't, he'll have to pay a fine to get him back."

I watched as the boy rode away on his bicycle at an unbelievable speed. It wasn't long until was out of sight. Whizz finished with the woman and came out to where I was. I told him that I had sent word for the owner to come get his animal. In a few minutes I saw the boy on the bicycle coming back up the street. He was smiling.

"I told him Mister Police what you said."

"Good. What's your name?"

"It's Willie, sir."

I saw a truck coming so I said, "Come on, Willie. Let's get us something cold to drink. After that ride, you look like you could use it."

We went in the store where they had a barrel full drinks buried in ice. I got Willie one and then one for my partner and me. I opened mine and went back outside. The fellow had the little animal in the back of his truck and was leaving.

I handed the drink to Whizz. "Let's get out of here."

We got in our patrol car and started down Hardy Avenue. Whizz started to laugh.

I looked at him. "What's the matter with you?"

"Herman was mad at you for what you told that boy to tell him."

"I just told him to tell him to come get his animal."

"That's not what the boy told him."

"What did he tell him?" I asked, turning up the drink and taking a big swallow.

"The boy told him you said for him to get his donkey ass up there and get that animal or you would put him in a pound and he would have to pay a fine to get out."

Coke spewed everywhere! I hadn't said any such thing! "He said what?" I finally asked after getting the coke out of my nose and wind pipe. I motioned for Whizz to pull over. I got out and wiped the coke from my face and shirt. I had blown the whole mouthful out on me. I got back in the car and started to laugh. I could just imagine how Herman felt when Willie delivered his message.

Joy Riding

One summer Whizz and I received a call from dispatch about a missing child. When a call goes out about a missing child, everyone sits up and take notice. Whizz and I had just changed from third to second shift. The call came in just as we finished eating, so it was still light out. We were told to see a lady on South Broad about a missing child. We were told that we should be on the lookout for a small child in a walker. When I learned the age of the child, a cold chill went down my back. I turned on the lights and was at the address in just a few minutes. The house was just past the old fire station, which was later turned into a nursing home for elderly people.

    I pulled up and we got out. There were several people in the yard. A young woman was screaming and they were trying to get her calmed down. Whizz went over to talk to her and finally got her calm enough to tell us what had happened. I listened with my microphone in my hand, passing information on to the other patrol car. It seemed that the woman had been in the kitchen cooking and the baby was in a walker in the living room. She said she could hear it rolling around. But then she realized it had gone quiet and she went into the living room to see what was up. That's when she found the front door was open and the baby and walker were gone. I looked at the door she said the baby in its walker was supposed to have gone out. There were two steps off the porch that the baby had to have gone down. I shook my head wondering how a baby in a walker had navigated those two steps. Since there was no sign of the walker, the baby had to have taken it with him. A motorcycle officer rode up and listened to what had happened. He stated he would search some of the side streets. The other car was down on Pennington Avenue so Whiz and I headed down South Broad.

East Main turns off to the right and goes down to the correctional institute. I did a slow cruise, with Whizz and I looking everywhere we thought a small child in a walker could go. We rode the area out and saw nothing. The other officers had not seen anything nor talked to anybody who had. I pulled onto the street off East Main that led to the Livingston Meat Packing Plant and stopped the car.

"Whizz," I remember asking, "what do you think?"

I remember he shook his head and asked, "How did a small baby in a walker get down those steps?"

I felt a cold chill run up my back. "Are you thinking what I'm thinking?"

"Yes. Someone had to have taken that baby. There's no way he could have come down those steps in a walker and kept moving."

I started to back out into East Main when I heard someone whistle.

"You hear that?" Whizz asked. "Someone is whistling at us. There!" He pointed to a man standing in the street waving his hands.

I pulled down the street to where he was. Before I could stop, the man started pointing toward the house. I stepped out to see what was causing the excitement.

"There, Officer," he said.

I followed his finger and could not believe my eyes, for there sitting in the yard in his walker, was a baby!

"We were sitting on the porch when down the street this baby comes rolling up," explained the man. "My boy ran out and stopped it from going in that ditch down there."

Whizz had walked over and picked the baby up out of the walker. He was kicking and laughing, having himself a ball. The man asked if we knew whom the baby belonged to. When we told him, he shook his head in disbelief.

With the baby and walker in the car, we let the other units know that we had the baby and were en route to his mother. After the baby was safely back in the arms of his mother, we traced the route that he traveled. We talked about that incident many times, but never could figure out how that baby got down those steps without tipping over. The distance he traveled was all downhill. How he managed to travel the distance he did without turning over or getting into the road remains a mystery. I have thought about it and always come up with the same answer: Someone up there was smiling down on him. He had to have guided the walker, because a two year old baby couldn't have!

American Hero

While walking a beat on Broad Street I became acquainted with a fellow who at that time was in janitorial work. In the morning a group of people washed windows on the store fronts before everyone else got to town. One such person was a small man who drove a van that said Henry's Janitorial Work on the side of it. Henry was the only name that I knew. I would pick up a cup of coffee and walk down to where Henry was washing windows so I could talk to him for a while before moving on. Then I left walking a beat and was assigned to a patrol car so I lost sight of Henry for a while.

Several years later, I ran into Henry again. My partner and I got a call to see a person in the east Rome area. When we arrived a small man was sitting on the porch wrapped in a blanket. It was warm weather and I wondered why he was wrapped in a blanket. After checking out, my partner and I walked up to the porch. As I approached I knew that it was Henry. He looked so pale and I knew that he was sick. I spoke to him and his face lit up.

"Officer Adcock, it really *is* you!"

"Yes Henry, it's me. How have you been?" I asked.

"Not so good," he said pointing to a chair and motioning for me to be seated.

I sat down facing him and asked, "What seems to be the problem that we can help you with?"

"It's some of the kids in the neighborhood. They started to write things on my fence and on the sidewalk in front of the house. There," he pointed.

I could see where someone had spray painted his fence. His house sat on a corner lot and we had come up on the front side. I motioned to my partner that I was going out on the street where I could see what was on the fence. There on the sidewalk was a huge swastika spray painted in white. On the fence were the words 'Nazi' and 'go back to your country.' I shook my head in disbelief at some of the other words painted there. I got my camera from the patrol car and took pictures of the fence and sidewalk. Why would anyone do this to someone? I couldn't understand. I went back to where my partner and Henry were and sat down.

I listened to him for a few minutes then asked, "Henry, do you know who did this to you?"

He replied, "Officer Adcock, I have no Iiea who would do such a thing. I've lived here most of my life and haven't had any problems with my neighbors. The people around me have been here for years."

"Have you seen anyone in the neighborhood who doesn't belong?"

"No," he said, shaking his head.

We got up to leave assuring him that we would keep a lookout for him.

Back in the car I pulled around to where my partner could see what had been written on the fence and sidewalk.

He shook his head. "I'd like to catch the one who did that to the old man."

We turned in the pictures along with a report and went back out on patrol. We kept a good check on Henry. As far as I know it didn't happen again. While talking to Henry, we had learned he was of German descent.

Some time later my partner and I were on the day shift and got a call to escort a funeral. We arrived at the funeral home and learned that the person we were going to escort was Henry. At the cemetery, after the cars were all parked, we backed off to watch the traffic. I was standing out side of the patrol car and heard the guns go off. Henry was getting a military send off. When the guns were fired, I got it a funny feeling thinking about the graffiti on his fence.

After all the cars had cleared the cemetery, we followed the Legion Honor Guard bus back to the Legion home. I knew most of the fellows that were in the Honor Guard. I asked them about Henry and what he had done in the Army and was told that he fought in the Pacific theater in World War II. He was among the first American soldiers that stepped into Japan when they had surrendered. One of the Honor Guards said Henry had more medals than most people have ever seen. Henry was an American Hero.

I look back and think about the things that were written on Henry's fence and try to imagine what kind of person could do that. Here was a man who fought to keep this country free so that someone could do this to him. The old saying "sticks and stones may break my bones, but words will never hurt me" comes to mind. True, sticks and stones will break your bones, but words can do as much harm to the heart of a person as broken bones can do to the body. Like so many other unsung heroes that are out there in this country, Henry was caught up in a hatred that he fought to keep this country clear of.

Before you put the bad mouth on someone, know them. The person you are putting down may be another American Hero.

Fore!

Early in my police career, Whizz and I were assigned to Beat Two—the East Rome area. At that time Rome only had two patrols cars running in the city. The shopping center at Maple and East Twentieth was experiencing a series of purse snatchings. We were told to check the area every time we had a chance. With only two cars covering the whole city, you can imagine how often we had time to check out the area.

On this particular day I had gotten into the patrol car. When we drove out of the parking lot, something rolled out from under the seat against my foot. I reached down and picked up a golf ball. I held it up and asked Whizz, "Did you lose your ball?"

He laughed. "I don't even know what side you are supposed to hit those balls on."

I held the ball in my hand squeezing it like an exercise ball. We headed toward Maple Street to check on the shopping center. When we got to Nineteenth Street Whizz turned and said, "Let's come in from the back side."

We drove down Flannery, then Hosea, and came in on the lower side of the shopping center. As we pulled in the lot, we heard a scream. "Stop him! He has my purse!"

Whizz accelerated but got blocked by people who ran out into the parking lot. I jumped out of the patrol car and ran after a man everyone was pointing at. I knew he had too much of a start on me for he was almost to the corner of the building. Not thinking about what I was doing, I stopped, took aim, and threw the golf ball at the subject. As he turned the corner he let out a yell and hit the ground face down. I ran but before I could get to him, he was up and around the back side of the building and out of sight. I looked but couldn't find him; he was gone. I picked up the purse from where he had dropped it and went back to where Whizz was getting information for a report.

I handed the purse back to the lady, who grabbed me in a big hug. "Thank you!"

We got all the names and information for a report then started a search of the area. The fellow must have lived close by and had managed to get inside. We asked radio to notify the hospital to let us know if anyone came in with an injury to the shoulder. I knew that the golf ball had hit him a good lick on his shoulder.

Whizz and I went back out on patrol keeping a lookout in the area in case the snatcher came back out. After supper, we checked back in and dispatch said the hospital had called. They had a man there with an injury to the right shoulder.

I looked at Whizz and said, "Yeah, I think that might be our man."

We headed over to the emergency room. A doctor met us and pointed us to a room. Whizz and I walked in and the subject almost fell out of the bed! We didn't say anything, just stood there. The longer we were quiet, the more nervous he got.

"Want to tell us about the shoulder injury?" Whizz asked.

"It won't do you any good to lie," I said. "We know how you got that injury to your shoulder."

The subject looked down at the floor. "What did you hit me with?"

"You, my friend," Whizz replied, "were hit by the best golfer there is!"

The doctor came in and told him nothing was broken, but he would be sore for a few days. Then he said, "Officers, you can have him."

The fellow stood up. We cuffed him and escorted him to the car. I put him in the back seat and got in with him. The doctor had come to the door and motioned for Whizz. Whizz went over and talked to him for a few minutes. When he got in the car, he was laughing.

"Know what the doctor wanted to know?" he asked.

I shook my head. "What?"

"He wanted to know if you threw that golf ball like you would a baseball!"

The next day when I came in, dispatch told me to see a fellow who worked in the drugstore in the shopping center at Maple and Twentieth Street. We left the station and headed for the shopping center wondering what we were wanted for. We asked the lady at the cash register if someone want to see us.

"I have something for the officer who threw the golf ball yesterday," she said.

Whizz laughed and pointed to me. "There's your golfer!"

She reached under the counter and took out a small box. She put it on the counter and said, "This is for you."

I looked at it, not saying a word.

"Open it." Whizz said. "Let's see what's in it."

I took the box and very carefully opened it. I stared for there in the box was a golf ball. I took the ball out of the box and saw a note folded up with it. I took the note and opened it and read: I found your weapon and was glad to return it. Keep up the good work.

I handed the note to Whizz. "No name," he said.

I looked at the lady behind the counter. She shook her head. "No name," she said.

"If you see the person who gave you the golf ball, tell them I said thanks."

I carried the golf ball back to the station that night and put it in my locker.

The next day Whizz came in and asked where the golf ball was.

"I put it in my locker," I replied.

He left and returned with two rocks and handed them to me.

"What are these for?" I asked.

"Well I've never seen you fire a gun, but I know what you can do with a golf ball. I give you these rocks for my protection!"

I didn't say anything, just picked up the rocks and asked, "Ready? Let's go!"

Railroad Ghost

Before Redmond Hospital or any of the others buildings on Redmond Road were built, it was a two lane road that ran though a wooded area from the last house on the road to the main gate at Battey Hospital. The last house on the road was there where the church now sits. There was nothing from that point to Battey Hospital but a railroad that ran to Berry Collage. It was there where the ghost was sighted.

At the time this incident took place, what is now the Chinese restaurant was called the Plantation House. Just below the Plantation House was a small drive-in. The drive-in was similar to the Dairy Queen of today. Whizz and I had picked up a hamburger and were sitting on the end of the lot eating. A car came down Martha Berry at a high rate of speed. Seeing us, the driver came sliding sideways on to the lot.

"What in the world is the matter with you?" Whizz asked as he got out of the patrol car.

"There!" The driver pointed. "Back there at the railroad!"

"What's back there at the railroad?" I asked.

"A ghost girl! I saw her!" The poor fellow was obviously agitated.

"Calm down and try to make some sense out of what you are saying," we urged.

After a few minutes the driver was able to get his story out. "I was coming down Redmond Road and when I got to the railroad tracks, I saw a girl standing by the side of the road. I stopped to see if she was having trouble and needed help. I rolled down my window and asked, 'do you need help?' She turned and looked at me and then started to float up the railroad. When I say float, I mean float. She had no feet showing beneath the edge of her dress. She floated about two feet above the ground. When I saw this I left there looking for you fellows."

He grew quiet and I looked at my partner with a smile on my face.

"Go ahead," he said, "and smile, but if you ever see what I saw you'll stop smiling."

I looked at him and said, "Follow us back out there and show us where this happened."

He shook his head. "Not me! I'm not going back out there ever again." With that, he got in his car and left.

I looked at Whizz and said, "Let's go ghost hunting!"

We pulled out on to Martha Berry and headed for Redmond Road. Once past where the houses ended the road became very dark since there were no street lights in this section. We came to the railroad tracks and stopped in the middle of them. I turned the spotlight on and shined it around the area, but never did see anything that looked like a woman with no legs. I took my flashlight and walked down the tracks looking around but still couldn't see anything, so I headed back to the car.

"See anything" my partner asked.

"No," I answered, "Nothing out there that I could see. Let's go to the gate house at Battey Hospital and see if they saw anyone out there on the railroad tracks."

We pulled up to the gate house and were greeted by one of the guards. We talked a while and then asked if they had seen anything. One of them said they had seen a car stopped at the tracks a short while before we arrived. The car had left in a hurry after stopping for a few minutes, the guard said.

Whizz and I left and went back to the railroad for a second look. We looked up and down the tracks but saw nothing. What the gate guard had said matched what the fellow in the car had said. We pulled out and went back on patrol.

The next morning at shift change, we asked the other officers it they had ever gotten a report of a ghost at the tracks. No one had, so we marked it down in our book as forgotten. But this would be one incident that would not go away and be forgotten, as we would soon find out.

Several weeks went by. One morning at three o'clock we got the call. Whizz and I had just gotten through eating at the Krystal on Shorter when we got the call to see the guards at the main gate to Battey Hospital. We drove down Division Street and found the guards outside talking to a man and woman in a car. We got out of the patrol car and went over to the group.

"Is there something we can help you with?" we asked.

"You remember a few nights back there was a ghost reported to you at the railroad tracks?" one of the guards asked.

Yes," I answered. "We remember."

"Then you have got to hear this," he said, indicating the couple in the car.

I looked the couple over and saw that they were middle aged. They looked like people who were not easily shaken up by things. When the man began to talk, I could see I was wrong for he was very excited. I tried to calm him down, and after a few minutes we were able to understand what he was saying. He and his wife had been driving down Redmond Road coming from Martha Berry when they saw someone standing on the side of the road in the middle of the tracks. Thinking it was someone who needed help, they pulled over and his wife rolled down the window. He said it appeared to be a young girl who stood in the tracks with her back to them.

He asked, "Do you need help?" She moved a few feet up the track away from the road. Thinking she could not hear him over the car motor, he turned it off. The man reported he got out of the car and came around in front of the headlights where she could see him. She moved another few feet up the railroad and stopped. He said he moved to the side of the car and asked again, "Do you need help?"

At this point in the story, the man's voice began to tremble. He stopped talking for a few minutes. We waited for him to continue.

"Officer, you're going to think I am crazy," he said. "I asked if she needed some help and she turned and looked at me. Her face had a white chalky look and when I looked down at her feet, I almost passed out. Officer," he said, "she had no feet! She was floating above the ground!"

He grew quiet and I looked at my partner. He nodded his head.

"Wait here," we told them, "while we go check out the area."

Whizz and I got back in the patrol car, drove to the tracks and shined the spotlight up and down them. Nothing. I got my flashlight and told my partner to go up to where the dirt road cut down to the tracks and wait for me. I began to walk up the tracks shining the light as I went. I saw the patrol car as my partner pulled onto the tracks and watched as he shined the light in the other direction. I reached the car seeing nothing that looked liked a floating girl with no legs. We drove back to the gate where the guards were still talking to the couple and let them know that we had found nothing that would indicate someone pulling a prank. The couple left and we went back out on patrol.

This, along with the other floating girl sighting, was discussed among the officers on the shift. Patrol cars became a common sight in that area for quite a while. What did the people see there at the railroad tracks? Did they see a ghost or was someone pulling a prank? The people involved in the sightings told basically the same story. They all saw a young girl with a white chalky looking face floating above the ground. All the people agreed on one thing: she was definitely floating above the ground and didn't have any feet.

Monkey Business

In the early 70s, my partner and I received a call that has brought a smile to my face every time I remember it. At that time the City of Rome Police only had two patrol cars running from three in the afternoon until seven in the morning. From seven in the morning until three in the afternoon there was only one car on patrol. Saturday nights could get a little hectic at times. There wasn't too much grass growing under your feet. We were kept running from the time we went on duty until the time we got off.

As I remember this particular night had been one of those nights when nothing was happening on Beat One. It was all happening on Beat Two. Dispatch gave us a call to a motel on Martha Berry. We were told to be on the lookout for a woman with a baseball bat running a naked girl down the street. That made my partner step on the gas to get there in a hurry. We pulled into the lot and the first person we saw was the woman with the bat. She had a man pushed up against the front of a car and was poking him in the stomach. I could see that the fellow who was getting poked with the baseball bat was not having any fun. I stepped out of the car and ordered her to thrown down the bat. Seeing how much fun she was having poking the fellow, I didn't think I wanted to play with her. She stopped poking and turned to look at me.

"Throw down the ball bat," I told her.

She acted as if she didn't hear me and turned and gave the guy one final poke. Then she walked over to a car and threw the ball bat in it.

"Officer," she said, giving me one of those big friendly smiles reserved for such an occasion. "Let me explain," she said. Again her face lit up with that big smile.

"You do that!" my partner said. "Someone has got some explaining to do."

"That worm!" She pointed to the fellow she had been poking with the bat. "That worm," she said again as she walked over and slapped him in the face, "is my husband!"

I stepped between her and her husband. "There will be no more hitting or poking, do you understand?"

"Yes officer," she said, again smiling sweetly. "Officer, that worm was supposed to have gone fishing with his buddy. I called my friend to see if she wanted to take in a movie only to find her husband, the fishing buddy, was at home. If he was at home then where was Harold?

"I knew that Harold wasn't fishing, so where was he and what was he doing? I got in my car and started to look the motel parking lots over and when I got here, I saw his car. There," she pointed, "the one backed in between those other two."

I turned and looked at the car she pointed at. I thought I was seeing things because there were three cars all the same make, model, and color. They were all backed in so you couldn't see the tags.

"How did you know that this car was your husband's car?" I asked.

She pointed to a tag on the front of one of the cars. I read the tag and a smile came to my face.

"Yes I know!" she said. "Wasn't he stupid?"

I motioned for my partner and he came over with Harold 'the worm.' With the understanding that he would leave his car and come back the next day, he could leave and go home. With both parties in agreement, they left and we went in search of the naked woman who was seen going down the street that ran beside the motel.

We drove slowly so we could look the area over. At the end of a short street we came to a park. There sitting on a bench was a young girl who had been crying. This was obviously the girl we were looking for. She sat on the bench with nothing on but a red shirt draped around her. When I got out and approached her, she jumped up and started to run. I told her to come back, that we would take her back to the motel to get her clothes. She hesitated but finally got in the patrol car. We carried her back to the motel and waited until she came out, got in a car, and left. We watched as she pulled out into the road.

As I started to pull off my partner said, "Did you ever see three cars just alike parked next to each other in a parking lot before?"

I looked at the three cars again and found it hard to believe. What was also unusual was they were *all* backed in to where you couldn't read the tag number.

I started to pull out again and my partner asked, "How did she know which car was her husband's?"

"There," I said, pointing to the car with the tag on the front. He started to laugh and I joined him because this was a funny thing that we were looking at. I can clearly remember what the tag said as if it happened yesterday instead of so long ago.

"Don't monkey with this monkey's monkey."

Take heed if that monkey is good at wielding a baseball bat!

Walk the Walk

Unless you have walked in the shoes of a police officer do not be so fast to criticize. Sometimes what you see happen with a police officer is not what you think you see. Nowadays it is easy to take pictures, but some of those pictures can be misleading. During my 32 years on the police force, we logged many complaint calls against officers. Some were legitimate but most were not. The complaint would be called in on just one part of an entire incident. The complainants rarely witnessed the whole situation. I can remember a few incidents where someone called in a complaint, but only had half the information.

One such incident happened to me and my partner Whizz. We received a call to the area that was called Romega Place back in the late sixties. The call was to a disturbance that was taking place in the yard of a house there. I was driving that night and when we pulled in, Whizz was on the side where the house was. I was on the side away from the house.

Whizz stepped out. Shots rang out.

"He has a gun!" Whizz yelled as he hit the ground.

I ducked down behind the car out of sight. I don't think the shooter ever saw me. He was concentrating on both Whizz and holding a woman in front of him. He had the gun against the woman head, yelling, "Stay away or I'll kill her!"

Whizz began to talk to him, trying to get him to put down his gun. Keep in mind this took place many years before we had SWAT teams. The officer on the beat had to handle any and all situations that came up.

I began to creep slowly down the street to where I knew the shooter couldn't see me. While Whizz kept him busy, I moved into a position behind him. As I got ready to make my move, the door to the house behind me opened and a man stepped onto the porch. The light from the open door fell on me, lighting me up.

"Get back inside!" I shouted at him. "Shut that door!"

I lay still on the ground waiting to see if the shooter had seen me. I could hear him telling Whizz he'd shoot the girl. I started to move toward a tree that would give me some cover. Then as I straightened up to make my move, the door opened on the porch again and the light lit me up. I won't repeat what I said, but the door shut with a bang as the man jumped back into his house. I sprinted to the tree using it for cover. It appeared that Whizz still had the shooter's attention and he hadn't seen me. I moved slowly onto the walkway making as little noise as possible. I moved to a small tree that stood beside the walkway. It was close to the guy and gave me some cover.

Once in position I told him to turn loose the girl and to put down the gun. I saw him stiffen in surprise and hold the woman tighter. I again spoke telling him to put down the gun.

Then in a big voice, I commanded, "Put the gun down NOW!"

That had the effect I wanted. He threw the gun down and turned the girl loose.

"Down on the ground! I ordered.

The shooter did as he was told and Whizz came up to cuff him. It was a cool night but the sweat poured down my head. We carried the guy to the station and locked him up.

We went back to that house when it got light enough for us to see. We looked the ground over to see where he had fired in the ground as he said he had. We couldn't find any place on the walkway or on the grass. We spoke to his wife, the woman he was holding hostage. She said he had fired at the patrol car. She stated that they were separated and in the process of getting a divorce. He had, according to her, come over and tried to force her at gunpoint to leave with him.

Since our shift was ending, Whizz and I headed back to the station. You might think that this was the end of it, but no. It wasn't long before we were summoned to headquarters to see the chief. When I got to the station Whizz was waiting outside for me.

"What's up?" I asked.

Whizz shook his head. "Don't know. I waited until you got here."

We were met inside and shown to a meeting room where the chief and a man and a woman sat.

"Be seated." the chief said. Turning to the man, he asked, "Which one was it?"

The man pointed toward me. "That one."

Then I recognized him. He was the neighbor who kept turning the porch light on me.

"What is it I supposedly did?" I asked.

"You told me to get back in my house and turn that porch light off. If I didn't, you said you'd shoot it out for me!"

The woman never spoke. She kept silent and looked bored.

"Did either of you tell him you would shoot the porch light if he turned it on again?" asked the chief.

I replied that yes, I said that.

"Did he turn the light on again?" the chief asked.

"No," I said shaking my head.

He then looked the man straight in the face and said, "You were lucky that wasn't me for I would have shot the light out the first time you turned it on me." The chief turned to me and Whizz. "You can go."

We left but stopped outside the door. We could hear the chief's voice and it sounded like he was giving the fellow an earful!

Whizz and I talked about what had happened the next time we were on duty. When the neighbor had turned that light on, he lit me up like a Christmas tree. I easily could have been shot. I think if Whizz hadn't had the guy's full attention and he had looked around and seen me, it would have been a different outcome. Whizz joked that he had to get himself a thinner belt buckle, one that didn't hold him so high in the air when he was lying on his stomach.

It's easy to look at a situation from the outside and say what should have been done. But it's another thing when you're actually in the situation. You can't be sure of your reaction. If you have never found yourself in this type of hostage situation, don't be so fast to criticize what a police officer does when he's the one in the situation. Get the facts and put yourself in the situation then see what you think you would done. Until you walk the walk and talk the talk, don't criticize. Remember, a policeman puts his life on the line for you every day.

Last Laugh

One time in the early 60s, Whizz and I were on patrol driving down Branham Avenue toward South Broad. Suddenly about a block ahead of us a naked man ran out in the middle of the street, jumped up in the air, and patted his butt at us. Whizz took out down the street as fast as he could go. I was watching the man as he ran down the middle of the street. I saw him one minute and the next he was gone. Whizz came to a stop and I jumped out of the car. He was nowhere in sight. It was dark and the streetlights didn't put out much light. I took my flashlight and walked around shining it in the dark places. A woman came out on the porch of a house and I asked her if she had seen which way he went. She shook her head and went back into her house. Whizz and I got back in the car and began to ride around but couldn't find him. We made several trips through the area but never did find him that night.

The next evening when we came in we asked the captain to put us back on the East side for we wanted to see if we could find that guy. We made a search of the area every time we got a chance before dark. We had no luck and checked out for supper. After we got through eating I took the wheel. Back to Branham we went.

It was just getting dark so I decided to come in off of South Broad. Just as I turned onto Branham, the same naked man ran out in the middle of the street. He jumped up in the air and patted his butt and began to run down the middle of the street. Whizz started to laugh as I gave the car the gas. I did not intend for him to get away this time! Just as I thought I had him, he ran out of the road and up the sidewalk. By the time I got the car stopped, he had disappeared on us again. I stood there looking around but saw nothing. The door opened at the same house as before and a woman came out on the porch.

"Did you . . .?" I started to ask but before I could finish the question, she turned and went back inside.

I walked over to where Whizz was standing. He was still laughing and I asked what was so funny.

"You didn't see his butt?" he asked.

"No," I said shaking my head, "what about it?"

"He was naked as a jay bird. He didn't have nothing on but a cut off sweat shirt!"

I went back to the car.

"You know what?" Whizz said. "That was a white man."

I turned and looked at him and asked, "Are you sure?"

"As sure as I can be," he replied, still laughing.

Again we kept a lookout the rest of the night but didn't see the guy again.

Whizz and I talked about the incidents the next evening during shift change. We again got the captain to put us on the east side for we were determined to catch him. Just as it began to get dark I got Whizz to put me out on South Broad. He drove on down Pennington and, with lights off, moved down to Branham and parked. I had told Whizz to give me time to walk up to where the fellow had been coming out into the street. Whizz waited a few minutes and then began to ease down Branham Avenue. I squatted down behind a hedge and watched as the police car approached.

Then from out of nowhere came a man with nothing on but a sweat shirt. He stopped in the middle of the street, jumped up and patted his butt at the patrol car. He then turned to run but I was standing within a few feet of him. He headed for the sidewalk but never made it. I let my flashlight fly. It hit him in the back of the head and he hit the dirt. I cuffed him.

Whizz and I hauled him to his feet. He wasn't hurt. We started him toward the car and he began to beg us to let him in his house to get some clothes.

"Where do you live?" I asked.

He pointed to the house where the woman had come out on the porch. We went up on the porch and saw where he had pulled off his pants. I picked them up and wrapped them around his head. We carried him to jail with his butt showing.

Whizz and I talked to him on the way to jail, trying to determine what his purpose was in running around in the street without his pants. He told us how he laughed because he had made fools out of us. I tried to find out how he had gotten away from us. Turned out he had his pants lying in a swing on the front porch and would squat down behind it and put them on. When I approached his front porch, he would stand up with a robe wrapped around him. He had looked like a woman in the dark. His voice was high pitched and he sounded like a woman. He said it was the funniest thing he had ever seen when he patted his butt at us. We explained to him when we were booking him how these two fools were getting the last laugh.

I remember the old saying: He who laughs last laughs best.

Run Shorty, Run!

After being assigned to a patrol car, my partner and I began the task of becoming familiar with the beats. Beat One covered East and South Rome and the lower end of Broad Street. Beat Two covered North and West Rome and the upper part of Broad Street. There was no Turner McCall Boulevard at that time. In between calls we would ride the streets to become familiar with them.

One day a call came in that sent us to the end of Branham Avenue at South Broad. The officers in car two were familiar with the location. They radioed us to be on the lookout for The Amazon.

"Look out for what?" I asked,

A laugh sounded over the radio. "You'll see!"

I looked at my partner. "Do you have any idea what they are talking about?"

Again I asked the other car what they were talking about. Silence greeted me and I didn't bother to ask again.

As we turned from South Broad onto Branham, I started to peer at house numbers. The house we were on the way to was on the right side of the street, putting it on my side of the car as we pulled up. Checking out, I opened the door and stepped out onto the sidewalk. The door to the house opened and the biggest form of a person I had ever seen appeared in the door. I waited until my partner came around the car before walking up to the house.

As we approached the front porch the subject shouted to someone inside, "You'll get straight now! The police are here!"

I stopped in my tracks. The voice coming from that huge form in the door was female! We walked up the steps where we could see what was going on.

"You called the police?" I asked, not taking my eyes off her huge form.

I stood six feet, but she stood above me. My partner who was shorter than me stepped back, amazed at what he saw!

When I say this woman was big, I don't mean fat; I mean *big*. She stood a good six feet, four inches tall and weighed in at about 220 pounds. She was muscled up like a man.

"What's the problem?" I asked.

"In there," she pointed, "my husband has been whipping up on me."

I looked at my partner and he looked at me shaking his head. I knew he was thinking the same thing I was.

"Let me and my partner talk for a few minutes," I told her. He and I walked out of earshot.

"What do you think?" I asked.

"I think if someone is whipping up on her, we had better get us some help! He'd have to be a giant to handle her!" he replied.

"I'll go in and talk to him. You keep her occupied while I'm in there," I said.

We rejoined the huge woman. "Which room is he in?" I asked.

"There," she said, pointing to a closed door .

I knocked on the door. "Police! Open the door!"

The door slowly opened and a voice said, "Come in, officer, but don't let her in!

"Open the door to where I can see you," I ordered.

Slowly the door opened and before he had a chance to do or say anything I dashed into the room with him. There, standing there in the middle of the room, was a man so small I thought at first he was a boy. He held a rag to his nose which was bleeding. His right eye was almost swollen shut.

He must have seen the surprised look on my face because he said in a voice that trembled, "Please officer! Don't let her hit me again!" He stood about five feet tall and couldn't have weighed more than a hundred pounds.

"Is that your wife?" I asked indicating the woman standing at the front door.

"Yes officer," he said, his voice trembling so badly that it almost gave away with him. "She used to be a good woman, but here lately all she wants to do is stay out at night in beer joints. I work at Anchor Rome Mills and when I came home, she tried to make me give her my paycheck. She took the last one and blew it in one night. I packed up my suitcase and was leaving. She grabbed me and started to beat me. My suitcase is strapped on my bicycle out there in the yard. Please officer, help me get to it! I'll leave and you won't have any more trouble out of me."

I looked at the little man who had a quiver in his voice and a tear in his eye. My heart went out to him. I said, "Come with me and do what I say."

He followed me outside where my partner stood talking to the big woman who was known as The Amazon. I kept little Shorty behind me, blocking him with my hand.

"There he is!" the Amazon screamed. "Let me at him and he won't whip up on me again!"

I put my hand on her shoulder and guided her away from the door, blocking it and turning her out of the way so Shorty could get by.

"Run Shorty, run!" I urged him as he scooted by. Then he was off the porch and grabbing his bicycle. My partner covered the steps so the Amazon couldn't get into the yard.

He too yelled, "Run Shorty, run!"

Little Shorty hit the street running as fast as his bike would carry him. A scream right beside me returned my attention to the Amazon, who was in my face. I held out my hand and she backed up toward the front door. She then called me a few choice names and slammed the door in my face.

I walked back out to the patrol car and got in. My partner and I left, headed down the street in the direction Shorty had gone. My partner started to laugh.

"What's so funny?" I asked. "Let me in on it because I could use a good laugh."

"That little man! Did you see how fast he moved when you said, 'run Shorty, run?' I thought there for a while the Amazon was going to get you!"

"She wanted to," I said, "but she knew better! I weigh over a hundred pounds. I'm nothing like little Shorty!"

I often thought about what happened that night. Back in those days there was no law against domestic violence. The injured party had to take warrants if they wanted to prosecute. Even if the injured party took out a warrant, the couple would be back together again after a few days. The warrant would be taken up and it would start all over again the next weekend. I don't believe she could have taken out a warrant for Shorty if the person who wrote the warrant had seen them together. The only place that Shorty would have hit her would have been on her big western belt buckle.

Hang On Cowboy

One day I remembered something funny that happened just after I was hired on at the police department. I was a rookie and as green as they came. I was assigned to ride with another officer whose partner was out sick. I had never worked with this officer before. It wasn't long before I was thinking, "Won't he ever stop talking?" He had talked continuously since I had gotten in the car.

We were driving down Maple Street when we got the call about a bull in the middle of Dean Street holding up traffic. I had learned from my partner's stream of chatter that he was an expert horseman. He also was a rodeo clown who kept the bulls from goring the cowboys.

I looked over at him and said, "This is right down your alley."

"I'll get that bull out of the road without any problem," he replied.

"Good," I answered, "for bulls are too big for me to play with."

We came up Nineteenth Street to Dean Street. The traffic was backed up all the way past Roy's Little Garden.

We turned on to Dean, but had to drive down the wrong side of the street. When we got near the Atlanta Dairies, I saw the bull. He stood in the middle of the street as if daring anyone to mess with him.

I stopped the car a few feet away and said to my riding partner, "There he is, cowboy! Go get him."

My partner opened the car door very slowly and got out. He stepped around in front of the car, then turned and walked back to the side. He did this several times. I didn't understanding what he was doing, so I asked him later, and he explained that he was getting the bull's attention away from everything but him. It worked because I had noticed that the bull had settled down and had quit bellowing. While he was bellowing, I wondered how in the world were we going to get that bull out of the street?

Then I saw something happen that I will never forget. My partner began to walk toward the bull as if he was going to grab him. Grab him he did, for the bull turned and began to walk down the street.

People had gotten out of their cars to see the action. I heard one woman say, "That officer is crazy walking up on that bull."

The bull was walking down the middle of the road when my partner ran up and grabbed him by the tail. That bull let out a bellow that sent the people hustling back to their cars. The bull started to run, but the officer held on and it looked like he twisted the tail. The bull turned and started into the driveway of the dairy. The officer was still hanging on. He had him turned but the twisting of his tail must have upset his stomach. With a big bellow he let loose with a load of bull dung. My partner saw it coming but couldn't get out of the way. It hit him full force where his gun belt was. The bull kicked up his back leg and ran down to a vacant field behind the dairy where he began to eat grass as if nothing had happened.

The officer stood still, looking down at his uniform and not saying a word. Then he turned and headed to a nearby service station. There where everyone could see, he took off his gun belt and took a bath with his clothes on. He paid no attention to anyone, just kept on washing himself down with the hose. I was busy trying to keep the bull in the lot behind the dairy. The dispatcher radioed me that the owner of the bull was en route to get him.

After taking the bath with his clothes on, my partner came back and waited with me. It wasn't very long before a truck pulling a horse trailer pulled into the lot. The driver got out, opened the door on the trailer, and reached inside for a piece of rope about ten feet long. He went to where the bull was eating and put the rope around his neck. He pulled on the rope and began to walk. The bull followed him like a dog would. The fellow loaded the bull into the trailer, closed the door, waved and drove off. It took a load off of my mind for I was proud to see him go. My partner had dried off enough to get in the car so I drove him to headquarters.

When we got there, it was shift change so you can imagine the heckling he took. If there was one thing I learned from the bull incident, it was that my partner was all grit. I also learned that if you must grab a bull by the tail, do so from the side and not from the rear! Oh, and if that bull lets out a loud bellow and kicks up his heels, run for cover!

Pants Up; Pants Down

It is not my intent to embarrass anyone with my writing. I may call a first name, but won't use a last name unless I clear it with the person first. This story involves some embarrassing situations, but it is a favorite memory! It involves one of the female officers who was on my shift. She didn't think it was funny when it happened, but later we both laughed at it.

A call went out to the car on the West Rome beat that there was a suspicious subject walking down the street. This was after dark and in a residential section. The female officer was on that beat, so she took the call and started en route. I told dispatch that I was close and would back her up. I turned onto the street in time to see the officer out of the car talking to the subject.

All of a sudden he grabbed his pants and pulled them down to his knees. The officer grabbed his pants and I heard her say, "Put your pants on!"

He held his pants up and she reached back to get her handcuffs. Then as quick as a flash he dropped his pants to his knees and let out a big laugh.

She grabbed his pants again. "Keep your pants up, do you hear?"

As I walked up, he muttered, "Yes ma'am."

Again she reached for her handcuffs and down went his pants. He let out a drunken snicker. I remember grabbing his shoulder just as the officer's temper began to show.

She ordered, "Keep your pants up or you can go to jail with them down!"

He looked at me and slowly began to pull up his pants. She

placed the cuffs on him and put him in the back of her patrol car. I told her I'd follow her in.

I must have had a big smile on my face, because she looked at me and said, "Lieutenant, don't you dare say what you are thinking!"

I must have laughed all the way to the jail. She was unloading the guy as I pulled in. I followed her into the booking station and waited until the jailer had him locked up. I noticed she hurried into the station and avoided talking to me. I kept thinking about the whole scene and it got funnier and funnier. I decided to wait for her in my car. In a few minutes, she came out.

I asked, "Are you all right?"

She nodded. "Yes, I'm ok."

I didn't mention the incident again that shift, but the next night I called her over to the side and asked, "Were you pulling that old drunk's pants up or down?"

She turned a shade of red, then started to laugh. "Did you ever see anything like that? Lieutenant, he'd laugh and down would go his pants. I would get them back up and before I could cuff him they would fall down again!" She was a good sport about the situation and took the kidding with a smile.

One thing you soon find out about police work is that there are very seldom two calls alike. I have heard many people in the department refer to a routine call. But I believed that to get into a routine was a bad thing to do. Treat *each* call with caution so you can go home at the end of a shift!

Another thing about police work: never let your battleship mouth overload your rowboat butt!

The Nude Burglar

A series of burglaries occurred in the area of East First and Turner McCall. The captain assigned my partner Larry and me to that area. It seemed that every weekend the buildings along North Broad and East First were burglarized. Complaints from the business owners were coming in. They wanted to know where the police were while the places were broken into. Saturday nights were usually so busy that we didn't get to slow down until early in the morning. When we finally were able to do a building check, it was too late because the burglar had struck and was long gone. At the time of this incident, there was a service station on the corner of Broad and Turner McCall. There was also a service station on the corner of East First and Turner McCall. The coke machines at these stations were regularly broken into and the money taken. Larry and I were told to stay close to these locations and catch whoever was burglarizing them.

When things slowed down enough for us to do a building check, we started down Milner Highway from Broad Street. We eased along trying to see the windows and doors of the buildings. We had passed the Rome New Tribune building when Larry said, "Look there on the sidewalk!"

I couldn't believe my eyes. Now, this was a cool morning and a jacket felt good, but there walking down the sidewalk was a man wearing nothing but a pair of shoes and socks. He ignored us as we approached. He walked slowly as if in no hurry. A nude man strolling down the street was not something we saw every day. I stopped the car and Larry got out, telling the man to stop.

The man continued to walk as if no one had spoken to him. I pulled the car in front of him as he stepped off a curb at East Fifth Avenue. He started around the car and I got out, hoping to cut him off. He smelled strongly of alcohol.

"Where do you think you're going?" I asked him.

"Home," he replied as he tried to step around me.

I took out my handcuffs and cuffed him. We placed him in the back of the car. He just sat there staring at me, not saying a word. I asked him his name. He just continued to stare at me silently, so we carried him to the police station where we locked him up. We never did learn his name.

Larry and I hit the street again and went back to the area that was having all the burglaries. We started a building-by-building check and everything was looking okay until we started down Spider Webb Drive and saw a door to a dentist's office was open. We got out to investigate and found stuff thrown all over the floor. We called the dentist, who came immediately. Some machines in the waiting room had been broken into.

Next, we went to a steak house that was where the parts store is now located. A door to that building stood open as well and a check found no one inside. We called the owner.

We then went to the service station there on the corner of Turner McCall and East First and found the owner opening up. We explained what we had found and asked him to check his place. He went around to the side where we found a broken window.

"He's been here," the station owner said.

Larry and I headed back inside to check things out and found nothing had been bothered.

The guy opened a door and said, "Down here is where he's been hitting me."

We followed him down a set of steps into the garage area. It must have been at least twenty feet down those steps. The owner walked over to the broken window and started to laugh.

"See that?" he asked, pointing to a ladder lying on the floor. "I did have the ladder sitting up and he would break the glass, open the window, and climb down the ladder. So I put the ladder on the floor last night before closing."

I looked up at the window, at least twenty feet off the ground.

Larry asked, "Are these your clothes lying on the floor?"

The station owner shook his head. "Not mine."

I looked at Larry and said, "We know who they belong to!"

We gathered up the clothes and found the pockets full of money. We couldn't understand what they were doing in the garage, though. We took the money-heavy clothes to the police station and showed the shift captain what we had.

He smiled. "I knew you two could get this guy if anyone could!"

Larry and I called in a detective and gave him a report one what we had and left the clothes with him.

All the way home that morning I tried to figure out why that man had left his clothes on the floor of the garage. That next night when I came in, I got my answer. He had broken in the garage before and dirtied his clothes climbing down the ladder, so this last time he'd thought he would fold up his clothes and put them through the window onto the ladder. Once inside, he figured he could put them on again. His mistake was not knowing the garage owner had moved the ladder. The burglar thought he was laying his clothes on the ladder, but they fell to the floor. When he found the ladder gone, he knew he couldn't reach the floor so he had to leave. That's when Larry and I found him cold and nude walking down the street. What made it bad for him was he couldn't deny the clothes were his. There in the inside pocket of his coat was his billfold with his drivers license in it! The burglaries in that area came to a halt and our captain gave Larry and me and "Atta Boy" letter.

Snake in the Purse

My practical joker partner Pete and I were working the third shift. At the time of this incident the police were dealing with an outbreak of purse snatchings at a shopping center on Maple Street. Women would come out of the stores and a male subject would run up, snatch their purses and then run up the street into a dark alley. The next day the purse minus the contents would be found inside a telephone booth. This telephone booth was the most popular place to leave a purse after emptying it.

By the time Pete and I came on duty, the stores were closed, so no purse snatchings. We would spend some time watching the phone booth to see if people would check the phone for leftover coins. Pete decided to see what would happen if he blew up a brown paper bag and left it in the telephone booth. It wasn't very long before a fellow came along. Picking the bag up, he looked around to see if anyone was looking. When he saw he was unobserved, he opened the bag and, finding nothing, he threw it down and went off muttering to himself.

We replaced the bag in the booth several times to see what would happen. This phone booth seemed to be a popular spot for everyone who came by while we were watching tried to open the bag.

The next night as we were pulling out from the station, Pete stopped and got a purse out of his car. Laughing, he said, "Now we are going to have some fun!"

What's in the bag?" I asked.

I'll tell you when we get to the telephone booth," he replied.

He was driving so we headed for Maple Street and the phone

booth. Not seeing anyone around, Pete got out and put the purse on the ledge underneath the telephone.

"Now," I asked, "what's in the purse?"

Pete laughed. "A snake!"

I sat there not believing that he had said "a snake." When I got over the shock of riding around with a snake in the car I asked, "What kind?"

"A black snake. They won't bite you! They're harmless."

I learned that he had paid some boys to catch him a black snake. He thought it would make a good joke to put the snake in a purse which he would leave in the phone booth. I couldn't believe he had done that just to pull a joke on someone.

I said, "Remind me to never look in anything you have."

"I wouldn't do you that way," he said.

We sat there longer than usual, but nobody came to the telephone booth. We didn't get any calls, so we settled in to wait. Then from out of the dark alley a real sharp-dressed guy came walking up to the booth. He reached in his pocket and pulled out some change. The door to the booth was closed, so he didn't see the purse until he was inside. We could see him looking around to see if anyone was around. We watched as he put the purse up by the telephone so he could see inside. When he opened the purse, the snake slithered out.

I have never laughed so much or so hard in my life as I did that night! He let out a scream of bloody murder and busted the door off the booth. He was jumping up and down and yelling at the same time. When the door fell off the booth, he hit the ground running and yelling. He was jumping up in the air grabbing his pants leg and running at the same time!

I looked at Pete. "Did that snake go up his pants leg?"

Pete was laughing so hard all he could do was nod.

After a few minutes of hysterics, we went over to the telephone booth. We moved the door out of the street and looked for the snake. The snake was gone but the purse was still there, so we put it in the car for another day. We watched the booth for the rest of the time we were on duty, but never saw the well-dressed fellow again. We never found out what happened to the snake, either. Did the snake crawl up his pants leg? I can't say, but by the way he acted led us to believe it did.

Crap Game

Back when I first joined the department, the older policemen would raid the local crap game when things got slow. You could sit back in certain sections of the city and it wouldn't be long before you could find a game. The locals moved their game from one house to another to throw the police off, but it didn't take long to figure out what house had the game. The house that had the traffic would be the one with the game.

I remember one game in particular that one of the old policemen carried me on. It was in the South Rome area. On a quiet Sunday evening just about dark he called the other car. We met on the lower end of Broad Street. The officer I was riding with asked the officers in the other car if they wanted to visit Hattie. Hattie, as I learned, was a woman who sold white whiskey and held crap games in her house. We sat there and they talked for a while figuring out the best way to approach Hattie without being seen. There was a side street that ran beside Hattie's house. You could go down there and come in the back of the house. We were to be the car that came in from the front while the other car came in from the back. My partner and I got into position while the other car moved to the back. The word from the other car came and we burst into the front of the house.

I had never been in a raid on a crap game before and had no idea what to expect. When the patrol car came to a stop we headed for the front door at a run. I got the surprise of my life when people started jumping out windows and anywhere else that a policeman was not blocking. We hit the back room where the table was set up. There were probably twenty or twenty five people in the house when we pulled the patrol car into the front yard. We managed to hold five or ten of them. Once they were cornered we began to look around. I was told to guard the people we had cornered. Being the youngest officer I was given the job that the others didn't want. I stood at the door. When one would move I would point my finger at him and shake my head letting him know that to move was a no no.

I noticed that one of the guys would lean over and whisper something to another man standing beside him.

"What's your problem?" I asked.

"Man," he said, "I've never seen such big policemen in my life!"

I have since thought about that night and have come to the conclusion that he was right. I was six feet tall and the runt of the crowd. My partner Darrell was six foot six. Joe and his partner were both six feet six if not taller.

There was money lying on the floor and I told the one who kept watching the big police to pick it up and put it on the table. In the scramble to get away, the white whiskey had gotten spilled over the floor. It was hard to breath with the fumes.

Hattie was booked along with several more and the rest were told to hit the road. No one had to be told twice.

Many years later another officer was riding with me and I got the idea to raid a crap game. I'll call the other officer Doug. Doug was a rookie who had been on the department only a few months. The shift captain put him with me and said, "Show him what policing in a car is like."

This particular day was a quiet Sunday evening. We had ridden around until it had begun to get boring. I remember thinking, "There has got to be something I can stir up to pass the time." It came to me find a crap game and break it up.

Off of Cotton Avenue there was a small lake next to the river. We knew that some of the locals would gather in an old bus that had been placed on the river as a fish house. The way the old bus was placed you could park and be on them before they could see you. I pulled in and explained to Doug what we would find. How many people would be there I had no idea. The locals had gotten smart because as we came around the corner of the bus, a lookout yelled, "Police! Run!"

They came from all directions hitting the bushes. I heard several splashes and ran around the bus to see people jumping in the river. Some were already climbing up the bank on the other side. We couldn't have caught anyone if we tried. I remember stepping inside and finding to my surprise a man at a makeshift table.

"What have we got here?" I asked.

He smiled and said, "Hello, officers."

Doug and I started to laugh. The man sat quietly not saying a word.

"Why didn't you run with the rest?" I asked.

"Couldn't," he said pointing to a pair of crutches in the corner of the bus. "Couldn't run, officer. Felt like it, but my crutches were on the other side of the room."

I looked at the makeshift table and asked where was the money I know they didn't have time to collect. The fellow was sitting in a position to where he couldn't have pocketed it before we got there. Doug came back in laughing and said, "They all made it across the river okay!"

I gathered up the money that was lying on the table and counted it. I handed the crutches to the man and said, "Come on, let's get out of here"

I watched as he took the crutches. I recognized him as soon as he stood up.

"I remember you!" I said. "They call you Limpy down on Hardy Avenue."

"That's me, sir," he said. "Old Limpy."

"Get out of here and go home."

He started slowly walking on his crutches.

"Just a minute," I said and he stopped, turning toward me. I dropped the money from the table in his shirt pocked.

He smiled. "Thank you, officer."

Doug and I got back in the patrol car and checked back in.

"Any luck?" the officer in the other car asked.

"They all swam the river," I replied.

I remember I started to laugh and Doug said, "What's funny?"

"Remember the money I put in Limpy's pocket? The money

they ran though the briar bushes and jumped in the river for? Well, the total amount that I took from the table and put in Limpy's pocket came to twenty seven cents!"

Angel

Now that I'm growing older and becoming an old geezer, I think a lot about things that happened in the past. Some memories are of the good times, and some are of the bad. Sometimes bad memories are forgotten, and sometimes they aren't. This particular incident I'm writing about happened many years ago and has become one of my most cherished memories.

I had worked a burglary in south Rome when I noticed my watch had stopped. There was a watch repair shop at the corner of Fourth Avenue and Broad Street, so I dropped by. The owner of the shop was standing out front when I arrived.

He spoke as I walked up. "Good morning, Officer Adcock."

"Morning, Gene," I answered. "I need you to take a look at this piece of junk," I said as I handed him my watch.

He took it and laughed. "Did you shake it?" Then he started walking toward the corner of Fourth Avenue. "I want to show you something."

I followed him to the corner where he pointed to an old fellow sitting on a bench across the street.

"Watch him," he said.

I watched the old man as he leaned forward and held still for a few minutes. Then he would lean back. He held a walking stick and would use it as a prop, leaning forward, then back. We both watched as he rocked back and forth.

"He comes to town about twice a week and sits on that bench. I've watched him before," Gene said. "He sits there for about an hour and then he gets up and goes up the street. I've watched him as he turns down Fifth Avenue." He held up my watch. "Why don't you go talk to him while I check your watch?"

"Sure, why not?" I answered. I started across the street, watching the old fellow rock back and forth. I approached the bench and he leaned forward, not realizing I was there. He was talking to himself. I stood by quietly and heard the word "angel."

When he grew quiet, I spoke, but he didn't move or answer. "Sir," I said, placing my hand on his shoulder. At that, he looked up and smiled. "Sir, are you all right?"

"Oh yes, Officer. I am quite all right." He moved over on the bench. "Have a seat and we'll talk."

I sat down and waited for him to say something.

"I bet you are wondering what an old man is doing sitting on a bench on Broad Street in the hot sunshine."

I didn't reply because I could tell he was ready to talk.

"Look up the street, Officer, and tell me what you see.

I looked up the street and saw cars and people.

"What do you see, Officer?"

"I see cars and people," I answered.

He grew silent as I waited. Then he said, "Let me tell you what I see when I look up the street. I see my Angel and she is just as pretty today as she was then." He paused, then continued softly, "I was in the Army when I first saw my Angel. It was here on this corner. I had started across the street when a siren began to go off. The streets were cleared and from up the street came the sound of music. I stepped out in the street to see what was happening.

"There, coming down the street, was a marching band and out in front of the band were three majorettes, and out in front of them was my Angel. She was the prettiest girl I had ever seen. I watched as she approached the intersection. She stopped in front of me and winked! In those days, girls didn't wink at boys. I just stood there as she went marching on down the street. I knew that the girl I was going to marry had just winked at me. I wasted no time in getting over to the football game!

"Officer, we met, courted and we married." He grew silent.

I waited until he turned back to me with tears in his eyes. "My

Angel got sick. The doctor said she had cancer. After that, it was in and out of the hospital. Finally, we carried her on what I knew was the time that we had been dreading. I was sitting by the side of her bed holding her hand. I felt a slight squeeze and she opened her eyes. I bent over and kissed her forehead and she smiled and winked. I felt her hand go limp and I knew that Angel was gone."

I watched the tears run down his cheeks as I stood up. He leaned forward, looking up the street and I turned and walked away. He no longer knew I was there for he was watching his Angel come marching down the street. Catching the light, I crossed the street and headed for the watch repair shop. My watch just needed a battery. I checked back into service and pulled away, taking a last look at the old man sitting on the bench.

As I turned up Fourth Avenue, I said to myself, "Girls didn't wink at boys back in those days, but Angels did."

Albuquerque

A few years back I went to a Fraternal Order of Police convention in Albuquerque, New Mexico with Wayne, another officer on the force. We left at night and got to Memphis Tennessee at about daylight the next morning. I made the loop and started across the Mississippi River. Wayne was asleep and I woke him up when we were over the middle of the river. When you compare what we call a river with the Mighty Mississippi, ours look like small streams. We crossed into Arkansas and began to look for a place to eat. This trip took place during the recession of the early 1980s so there weren't too many cars on the road. After we ate we got back on the interstate with Wayne driving. We were in Wayne's silver Corvette. With my six foot frame, it was hard to get comfortable enough to sleep, but I managed to after having been awake all night.

When I woke up I didn't have any idea where I was. I could see rice paddies on the side of the road. I just guessed that they were rice paddies for they looked like the pictures of paddies I had seen. I remember asking Wayne, "Did you drive us all the way to China?"

He laughed and said, "Go to sleep on me and you just might wake up in China for real."

I remember looking at my watch and seeing that I had been asleep for several hours. I sat back and took in the scenery. We drove all day, only stopping to eat. By Oklahoma City, we were getting tired so we stopped and got us a motel room for the night. We ate and after a bath I went to bed. I can hardly remember my head hitting the pillow.

The next morning early we were on the road again. A good

night's sleep left me feeling refreshed. I sat back and took in the scenery. Wayne and I laughed about traveling down Route 66 in a silver Corvette just like the one on the T.V. series "Route 66." Cars would pull up beside us and the people would look to see if we were the actors in the TV show!

This one car with two people in it pulled up beside us and the driver revved up his motor. He made a motion like he wanted to race. Wayne was driving. He just held it at the legal speed limit. The driver of the other car stepped on the gas and pulled away from us at about twice the speed limit. Wayne just rolled along. We hadn't gone too much further before we saw a state trooper ahead with someone stopped. As we passed, I saw it was the car that had tried to get Wayne to race. We got a big laugh out of that!

We arrived in Albuquerque that evening and checked into our motel. After resting for a while we went down the street to a cafe to eat. As we left the motel we saw a man lying on the side of the street in a grassy era. He lay still and we laughed, thinking he was an old drunk. After we ate we headed back to the motel. The man still lay in the grass. Police cars and people were all up and down the street but no one seemed to pay attention to the guy in the grass. One of us made a remark to the effect if that was Rome he wouldn't lie there long.

Early the next morning, Wayne and I headed to the cafe for breakfast and the first thing we noticed was that the man was still on the grass. He appeared to be in the same position that he had been in the night before. After breakfast we headed for the convention center and were there all day. When we returned that evening the man still lay on the grass. We began to wonder if he was dead!

The next day was like the day before. We started the morning off with breakfast and wondering if the fellow in the grass was dead. We had some free time so Wayne and I toured old Albuquerque. Old Albuquerque was where the town first started and it still looked like something out of the past. It was full of shops with just about any kind of Native American jewelry. In an area set aside for traders, the Native Americans spread their jewelry out on the grass. You could watch them make it. There was this one old man who stood out from the rest. Wayne and I walked up and watched for a minute. I noticed that the old man look straight at me.

I stood quietly for a few minutes, not saying anything, just watching him. He was rubbing on a ring and acting like he didn't know I was there. I have never known what made me say what I did, but a smile came to his eyes.

I said, "Grandfather, you have the most beautiful jewelry of them all."

He then said, "You come from the land of the Cherokee."

"I come from the state of Georgia," I said.

"Yes," he answered, "from the land of the Cherokee."

I stood silently waiting for him to say more, but he only looked at me. I saw that he wasn't going to say anything else, so I moved on looking for Wayne.

With the convention over, Wayne and I went back to the motel to pack and get ready to start home the next morning. The fellow was still lying on the grass. Wayne went to talk to some of the other officers from Georgia. He hadn't been gone long before he came back to the room.

"Come with me," he said. "I want to show you something."

I followed him out to the street. "Look there," he pointed.

I couldn't believe what I was looking at. There, wobbling off down the street, was the fellow who had lain on the grass ever since we'd been there. We watched him and laughed. Our question was answered. We knew he wasn't as dead as we had thought! Why the police let him lie on the street as long as they did was a mystery to us. I think he got up at night and slept there during the day.

I will always remember the old Native American man there in Albuquerque. His deep penetrating eyes and the look on his face told me that if you could sit and talk to him, you would leave a smarter person than you were before.

Blue Angel

Sometimes when you least expect it, a memory will pop into your head. This happened to me a few years back. I suddenly remembered a call from dispatch about a runaway girl. I told dispatch that I was close and would back up the other officer. The address was in the East Rome project. It was a spring morning and it had been raining, but now the sun was out.

The other officer and I arrived at about the same time and walked up to the door together.

The officer remarked, "I believe it going to be a beautiful day after all."

I looked up at the sky filled with sunshine and replied, "I believe you're right!"

I stepped off to the side of the door and knocked.

A slurred voice called out, "The door's open. Come in!"

I pushed the door open, revealing the interior without exposing us. I saw a very large man sitting in a chair drinking beer. I stepped inside so I could see the rest of the room. Standing in the kitchen door was a woman with two small kids. The woman probably didn't weigh more than ninety pounds. The two kids beside her were a boy and a girl. The little girl had on a pair of panties, nothing else. The little boy was wearing a pair of shorts but no shirt. Neither wore shoes. It was still too cool for that type of clothing.

I motioned to the other officer to engage the big man in the chair in conversation. I wanted to get the woman away from him, so headed for the kitchen. A cracker box was on the table with cracker crumbs sprinkled around. I pointed to the table and the cracker box.

"It's all we had to eat, officer," the woman explained.

"You mean a few soda crackers is all these kids have had to eat?" She nodded yes.

"Where does he work?" I asked, pointing to the fellow in the other room.

"He doesn't," she replied. "I do the work and he takes the money and drinks it up."

I walked over to the refrigerator and opened the door. The shelves were bare.

"How do you get along," I asked, "if he drinks up what money you make?" I looked down at the two small children who were watching my every move.

The little boy tearfully asked, "You going to take my daddy and put him in jail?"

I smiled down at him. "No son, not today." But I was thinking *I'd sure like to!*

I turned back toward the room where the other officer was still talking to the man. The woman tugged on my sleeve and I turned to look into her eyes. She was trembling and her voice had a quiver in it.

"It's him," she whispered, "what called the police because my oldest daughter went to my mother's."

"How old is your daughter?" I asked.

"She fourteen. He's her stepfather. When he's like he is now, she can't stay around him."

"What are you telling him about me?" the man yelled from the other room.

"Nothing!" the woman yelled back. But to me she whispered, "Please help me and my kids get out of here!"

"Where will you go?" I asked.

"I don't know! To my mother's, I guess."

"I can only take your kids out; you'll have to get out on your own.," I explained to her.

"If they take my kids, will I get them back?" she cried.

I explained we would get a representative of child services out to talk to her about her options, then radioed dispatch about the request.

The big guy hollered out, "I heard you on that radio! I want you out of my house!"

I went to stand in front of him and wondered how anyone could let himself get in the shape he was in. He wasn't much over five feet five and I would say he weighed close to 300 pounds. A case of beer with a few empty bottles sat in front of him.

"You, he said again in a slurred voice, "I want you out of my house!"

"I'll get out of your house when I'm ready," I retorted, then turned to the woman.

I walked her over to the stairs that led up to the bedroom. In a low voice I told her to go up and pack some stuff for herself and the kids because they wouldn't have time once children services got there. I went back over to the big guy.

"I don't think I like you!" He pointed his finger at me.

I didn't reply because the woman from child services arrived just then. I explained what we had. She and I then went into the house to talk to the woman and when they got ready to leave, I escorted the women and kids to the door.

I thought the big guy was getting up to cause trouble, but he only reached for another beer and watched quietly as his wife and kids left.

When everyone was safely outside, he spoke up in a slurred voice. "I shall remember you!" He jabbed his finger at me once more.

I just closed the door on him and looked over at the other officer who was grinning.

"What?" I asked.

"Lieutenant, I don't believe that fellow liked you!" He jabbed his finger at me and laughed. As I got back into the patrol car, I thought about how it had turned out to be a pretty day after all.

Several years passed. I forgot about the incident until one day I checked out with my shift Sergeant to have supper. The waitress came over to take our order. I noticed that she was reading my name plate.

"It *is* you!" she exclaimed. A big smile lit up her face. "I've tried to remember your name, but couldn't!"

"Do I know you?" I asked.

She replied, "You are my angel in blue."

My sergeant started to laugh. "I've heard him called everything but not an angel!"

Our waitress then went on to explain who she was and the memory came back to me. She showed me pictures of the two little ones and of the daughter who had run away that day. She explained that the oldest girl was in college and the two others were A students. I could tell that she was now doing all right. I didn't ask about her husband because I thought that part of her life was better off left alone.

We left the cafe with my Sergeant calling me an angel. In all the years I was on the department, I was called a lot of names. This was the first and only time I was called an Angel. A Blue Angel at that.

Streakers

I remember several amusing streaker incidents from the time when streaking was the going thing among young people. One incident that someone called was about a naked man running up Martha Berry Highway. The caller stated the streaker would leave the Elstonian Motel out past the underpass at John Davenport and run to another motel, the Oak Hurst, at the top of the hill. Cars were dispatched to the Elstonian Motel.

I was coming in from toward town and saw the guy running in the center of the road toward me. I positioned my car in the center of the road, forcing him to turn into the Motel. A group of bushes lined the side of the driveway in front of the rooms. I eased my car over which forced him to run into the bushes. As I was getting out of the car, two more police cars pulled in. One of the cars was driven by a female. The streaker was cuffed and placed in her patrol car and she transported him to jail.

The second streaker incident involved someone streaking through a shopping center parking lot. I pulled my car into a dark space and waited. Nothing happened. I was about to give up when a knock on the back of my car made me turn and look. From out of nowhere, two naked females ran by my car. I was so stunned I sat there and watched as they rounded the corner of the shopping center and disappeared down a side street. I finally realized what had happened and took off after them. I drove down the street but didn't see anyone. I drove back up to the parking lot, stopped the car and stepped outside. This was early in the morning somewhere around two o'clock. Nothing was moving. I got back in the car and shut the door and then from out of nowhere the two naked girls ran from the other end of the lot, stopped, looked at me and across Shorter Avenue they went. I have no idea where they went. By the time I got to the other end of the parking lot they were nowhere in sight.

There was one incident that I remember which took place on East Third Avenue. I came off Glen Milner by the old Girls High and turned up East Third Avenue toward Broad Street. I was driving slowly looking at the houses as I went. A friend of mine who lived in the area had asked me to keep a check for him because he had heard a lot of loud noise at night.

I was even with the old Boys High at the top of the hill when I saw someone run across the street. I eased on down with my lights off and approached the intersection of East Second Street and East Third Avenue. Then it happened. Not one but two naked females streaked across the street in front of the patrol car. I stopped. Bringing up the rear was a girl who was so fat she couldn't run, so she calmly walked across the street and disappeared among the houses. I called into headquarters to request the patrol car on that beat ride though and keep a check.

This next incident happened not too long ago. My wife and I had been to town and were coming back out Highway 53 toward Veteran's Memorial Drive. The light caught us so we were sitting at the intersection when from out of nowhere a naked male ran in to the intersection. A car almost hit him but he zigzagged though the traffic while everyone sat and stared. He cleared the intersection and ran in the woods. A car pulled along the side of the road and the streaker ran out and hopped into it. His being naked and it being the summer made me wonder how he and those little red bugs known as chiggers got along.

I know the Martha Berry Highway streaker was barefooted. I wonder if the shopping center and East Third Avenue streakers were barefoot as well. East Second Avenue and East Third street were full of loose gravel and other types of dirt. I don't remember seeing their feet in the street lights. I don't remember seeing the feet of the streaker at the intersection of Veteran's Memorial Highway and 53, but if he was barefooted, he had some hot feet running on that asphalt!

I have always wondered if you wear shoes when you streak, or do you run totally in your birthday suit? I know that the next streakers I see, I'll look at their feet to see if they are wearing shoes!

UFO

I worked too many night shifts to count, so naturally I know all about looking up into a clear night sky and seeing something you can't explain. These things are called UFOs. There is nothing that says you will see little green or gray men, but if you look up long enough, you *will* see things moving in the sky. I've had three such experiences.

One such incident happened one night while I was on patrol. I had stepped outside of the car to have a smoke. I was over behind the levee at the ball field. It had been one of those nights when everything seemed to explode. I lit the cigarette and as I was putting the lighter in my pocket, I saw a bright light coming up the river. As it approached I could see that it was in the sky above the water. Where the river makes a bend, the mysterious light came to a standstill. I watched, fascinated. As suddenly as it arrived, it left, shooting straight up at a high rate of speed. What it was, I don't know. I do know that it could travel at a rate of speed that seemed impossible. It could also fly straight up. The light was out of sight in just a few seconds.

I had another memorable UFO experience. One night I was called to see a patrol car on Dean Street. When I arrived the officer was outside his car.

He came over to me and said, "Lieutenant, I just saw a UFO!"

I laughed and said, "I just saw Godzilla on Broad Street!"

"Lieutenant I'm serious! I saw something up in the sky that looked liked a ball of fire."

I turned off the motor and stepped outside with him. "You

know if you go back to headquarters and tell them what you saw, you'll be laughed at."

"I can't help it," he replied. "I know what I saw."

As I turned to get back in to the car, he shouted, "Lieutenant, up there!"

I looked up and sure enough, there in the sky was a bright light that looked as big as a football field. It was moving at a fairly fast pace. No motor could be heard. I jumped in my car, started it, and pulled out onto Dean Street. I could see the light over Saddle Mountain. I drove to the top of Saddle Mountain on Rockmart Road and could still see it in the distance. Then it disappeared from sight and I called the dispatcher to ask it anyone else had reported it. Yes, calls had come into police headquarters reporting a bright light in the sky. It was also seen over Rockmart that night.

One night, I was sitting in the house when my wife called me out to the sun room.

"Look up there!" she said, pointing up in the sky.

A light was moving around in the sky. I watched it move up, down, and all around. It would stand still and it appeared to have a brighter light coming from under it. At times the light would seem to pulse. It would go up and then it would shoot straight out.

Grabbing my video camera, I began to record it. I recorded it for a while from the sun room and then decided to go out in the yard. From the front yard, I could shoot across the top of the house. I wanted to get the top of the house in the video for reference so if people saw the video, they would know the light was high in the sky.

I was so into taping that I failed to see my cat walk up. I was in my pajamas with house shoes on. Not getting the attention she wanted, my cat decided to climb my leg. Now imagine watching a UFO and suddenly a cat grabs you by the leg with her claws! I can't say how high I jumped or the word I yelled. I will say that it ended my filming of whatever was in the sky!

Now I ask you: were some of these flying saucers manned by little green men? I can't say that I have ever seen any green or gray aliens. Whatever it was that I saw was always so high in the sky I couldn't see who was flying. If there are aliens flying around our country, why don't they stop off and visit for awhile? They might want to stay if they see what a great country we have.

Unidentified Flying Objects *are* out there. Stay up some night and watch the sky. You may get the surprise of a lifetime.

Lonie and the Police Department's bicentennial patrol car

Mud Bath

Here's an incident that happened a few years prior to my retirement. Rome, like any other city, has its Lovers' Lanes and we used to keep a good check on them. Most older people don't know where they are, but the younger generation knows. Lovers' Lanes are always full on the weekends. One of the most common ones was behind the levee at the Little League ball field. Couples could pull over on the back side and be in a position to see if a patrol car came in the gates. By the time the patrol car could get to where they were parked, the couple could be over the levee by the American Legion and long gone.

This incident happened on a Saturday night. It was one of those busy nights when for several hours straight, we ran from one call to another. Finally things calmed down and I decided to stop at the convenience store on Shorter Avenue across from the American Legion. You could get a good hot dog there and some sort of goody to go with it. After eating my hot dog, I left the store, pulled across the road, rode around the American Legion, and then across the levee onto the ball field. I was driving around the road when I realized that I hadn't turned on my lights. I started to turn them on when I saw a car parked on the back side next to the river. I eased around until I was behind the car, then turned on my lights. When the lights came on, I saw movement in the car and heard a noise like a door shutting. I got out and moved into a position to see the occupants of the car. There was only one person in the car and she sat behind the steering wheel. I knew that there had been two people in the car.

"Step out of the car," I said and she opened the door and got out.

I moved over and took the keys out of the car so that no one could jump in and take off.

"Who's here with you?" I asked.

She didn't answer so I asked again.

No response. The woman just stood still and stared at me.

"Move to the front of my patrol car and stand against the rear of your car," I said.

She hesitantly moved between the two cars. I took a good look at her. She was in her early thirties and dressed fit to kill. She looked like she had stepped out of a fashion magazine.

"Let's get serious," I said. "I know there was someone in the car with you."

I requested a back up. I didn't want to take a chance that someone was hiding out in the bushes with a gun waiting for me. The woman still had not answered any questions. I saw a patrol car come though the gates in the levee. I knew that once the other officer got there, I would find who had jumped from the car. The patrol car pulled up and the officer got out. I told him to watch the woman while I looked for the person who had jumped from the car.

I began a search of the river bank. It had been raining earlier in the evening so the banks were slick with mud. I didn't see anyone so I began to shine the light in the willows that grew in the water. At this spot they had the edge of the water covered and I couldn't see the edge of the bank. Then I saw where something or someone had slid down the bank and into the river.

I went back to where the other officer was and asked him to pull his car to where the spotlight would hit the water. When the car was in position, I turned the spotlight on and lit up the edge of the bank where the willows were. There, hiding in the willows, was one of the muddiest people I had ever seen. He didn't have on a shirt. He had taken it off and used it to wipe his face. There was mud from the top of his head to his waist. How he could have gotten that much mud on himself was a mystery.

"Come on out," I told him, but he stayed put. I put the spotlight on him and said, "Get up this bank and out on the road before those muskrats find you." He still didn't move.

The other officer had walked over to me. I asked, "Do you remember that fellow who was fishing down here the other night and fell in the river?"

The other officer picked up on it and loudly said, "You mean the one that got his toes eaten off by the muskrat?"

Still no movement from the willows.

"Hold the spotlight on him," I said and moved out of the fellow's sight. I picked up a rock, walked behind the patrol car, and threw it out in the water behind him. Then I hurried back to where the light was.

"Did you hear that?" I asked the other officer.

"Muskrat!" he replied.

I threw another rock within a few feet of the guy in the water and he let out a yell.

"Help me!" he cried. "Don't let them rats bite me!"

"Get out of the water. They won't follow you."

It looked like he got up on top of the water and ran out on the bank only to fall and slide back in. I threw another rock in the water close to him and he let out another yell and hit the bank running. He was almost to the top when his feet went out from under him sending him back into the water. Another well-placed rock and he hit the top of the bank and didn't slow down until he was in the middle of the road.

I put the spotlight on him and will never forget what I saw. He had on a pair of shorts that were plastered to him with mud. He looked as if he was made out of mud. I remember that I had to walk off so he wouldn't see the expression on my face. The other officer was shaking with laughter. He went over and looked down the bank where this guy's clothes and shoes were. I watched as he slid down and pulled them from the mud. To my amazement he made it back up to the road without falling down. I watched as the guy pulled his muddy pants on. Mud oozed out from in the pants leg as he pushed his feet in them. He poured water from his shoes and slid his feet in.

Then he turned to me and asked, "Officer, may we go now?"

"Sure," I said handing the car keys to the woman.

He started around the car to get in, but the woman jumped in and locked the doors telling him, "You aren't getting in my car with that mud on you!" As she rolled up the window, she said, "Goodbye! Have a nice day." With those words she started the car and pulled off.

The guy stood in the middle of the road watching as she went though the gates under the levee. She was a lot older than he and was wearing a wedding band. He had no ring on his hand. I looked at the other officer. He smiled and shook his head. The boy started to walk toward the levee. The other officer and I had a discussion about what had happened as he disappeared over the levee behind the American Legion Hall.

I left the area and crossed the levee at the Second Avenue bridge. I was on Broad Street when dispatch said to see a man at the convenience store at the trestle on Shorter Avenue. I told them I was en route and headed that way. I could see the young man, mud and all, talking to a man at the door of the store. I pulled in, stopped the car, and got out.

I smiled at him and said, "We meet again."

He didn't say anything but the man he was talking to did. He began by saying, "Officer, my son was taken by force and thrown in the river by a carload of boys."

I stopped him and, looking at the boy who hadn't said anything, said, "Tell him what really happened."

The boy dropped his head and told his father the truth.

His father walked over to his car. "You shouldn't have lied to me," he said and started to drive off.

"Hey, what about me?" the boy asked.

"Walk home. It will do you good. I don't need that mud in my car." He pulled out in the road and left him standing there.

The boy turned to me. I could see that he was about to cry.

"Where do you live?" I asked.

"On Burnette Ferry Road," he replied with a quiver in his voice.

"Come on, let's find something that I can put over my car seat."

With a box cut to fit the seat and floor, I headed for the Burnette Ferry Road. The young man showed me where he lived and I pulled over and got out to open the door for him. He gathered up the box, placing it on the side of the road. Making sure that there was no mud on the seat, I closed the door. He turned to leave.

I asked him, "Did you learn anything from what happened to you tonight?"

He stopped then said, "Yes Officer, I did."

I waited for him to tell me what he had learned, but he was walking toward his house. "So, what did you learn?" I called after him.

He turned and said, "Officer, I learned to never park the car so close to the river again." Then he went on to the house.

I rode back up the road laughing at his answer.

Cemetery Lights

The first time I came in contact with anyone concerning the lights in the cemetery was back in the late sixties. I was assigned to a patrol car with Whizz. We had turned down Branham Avenue there beside Myrtle Hill Cemetery was a car stopped in the driveway that led to Coosa Country Club. We watched the car as we approached it. The occupants were outside sitting on the hood. They sat still as if not paying attention to us.

"What do you make of it?" I asked Whizz.

"They seem to be watching the cemetery," he replied.

I pulled in beside the car and then got out and walked over to them. "What's up fellows?" I asked. "What's going on?"

"Nothing officer," one of them said. "We just parked here to watch the cemetery lights."

"You're doing what?" Whizz asked.

"Watching the cemetery lights."

"You are watching lights in the cemetery?" I repeated to make sure I had heard him right.

"Yes," he answered and pointed toward the top of Myrtle Hill.

I looked at the top of the hill and sure enough there were lights that seemed to be moving around among the graves.

I looked at Whizz. "Come on! Someone is in the cemetery."

We hopped back in the car and drove back to South Broad and onto Myrtle Street where the gate to the cemetery was located. I got out and checked the gates, only to find them locked. No one had been though them that night.

I got back in the car telling Whizz that they were locked. We drove back to the boys who were still sitting on their car.

"Find anything, Officer?" I remembered one of them asking.

"The gate was locked," I said.

"I know," he said. "We checked before we came around here to watch."

Whizz and I sat there with the boys for awhile watching the lights and came to the conclusion that they were coming from car lights. Where the cars were we didn't know. We never did figure out where the lights came from. We would stop every so often and watch them while working the third shift. Then one day we realized we hadn't see the mysterious lights in awhile. Time passed and I forgot them.

Many years later after I had become a shift supervisor, the cemetery lights came back. I remember the night I saw them again as if it just happened. It was a quiet night— the kind that gets boring after a while. I had been riding out to the buildings on North Broad and had pulled in the shopping center. I got out to stretch my legs when suddenly a car came speeding across the bridge there by Troy's Bar B Cue. He turned down North Broad and drove into the parking lot.

Pulling up next to me, he exclaimed, "Officer, there are lights moving around in East View cemetery! I saw them as I came by."

"Where were the lights?" I asked.

"In the middle of the cemetery!" he said.

"I'll go check," I said, getting back in to my patrol car. I called dispatch, told them what I had, and asked for another car for backup.

I arrived at the main gate of East View Cemetery in just a few minutes and turned off my lights. I stopped for a few seconds but didn't see anything. I began to ease up the driveway with my lights off. I drove across the cemetery to the other side where the church is located.

In a few minutes one of my patrol units came over the hill from the other side. I blinked my light and he came over to me. This was one of my new officers. I told him about the lights.

He started to laugh and said, "Cemetery lights? Lieutenant, you never heard of them?"

Then I remembered the Myrtle Hill incident from years before. I started to laugh and said, "You believe there are lights that dance around in the cemetery at night?"

"I know there are. While growing up, we used to go to cemeteries and watch them," he replied.

"I don't see any now, do you?"

"No," he said, "but at certain times of the night you can."

I laughed and said, "Sure and I bet you can see people out there holding the lights!"

"Laugh if you must," he said, "but they're there!"

I pulled out onto road still laughing.

I soon forgot the lights in the cemetery—until one night I was checking out a building across the road from the gate to the cemetery. I saw a light in the cemetery and went to check, riding the cemetery from bottom to the top. I didn't see anything. On top of the hill where the office and maintenance building was located, I stopped where I could get a view of the entire cemetery. I turned my lights and motor off. I got out and stood outside my car when there in the middle of the cemetery I saw the lights! At first it was one light, then two. I watched as the lights seem to bounce around from place to place. I was amazed for I knew that there was no one else in the cemetery. I must have stood there for several minutes before getting in to my car and moving in the direction of the lights. Stopping where I had seen the lights, I shined my spotlight over the area. Nothing. I drove back to where I had been before. I got out again and waited and sure enough, the lights came back! I must have stayed there fifteen minutes watching the lights.

The night was quiet and not too much was going on, so I thought I would have some fun. I had a female officer on that side of town so I radioed her and asked that she see me at the cemetery. In a few minutes I saw the patrol car go down the road and turn in where the church was. I told her to see me on top where the office was. I watched with a smile on my face as the patrol car started up the road to the top of the cemetery. The lights had disappeared by the time she reached the top. I walked over to the car and began to talk to her. I told her about the lights and could see that she was uneasy sitting there.

"Come here," I said, motioning for her to come with me.

Rather hesitant she got out and came over to where I stood. I pointed to where the lights had been and said, "You need to keep a watch in that area there."

I wanted the lights to show again while she was there but they didn't. I could see that she was nervous so I told her to go ahead. I watched as she left the cemetery.

I sat many a night and watched the cemetery lights trying to figure what they were. I never found any explanation for them. Their occurrence was something that I accepted as being here without a reason. I wouldn't advise anyone to go to a cemetery after dark. There is a law against being in the cemetery after dark. If you are among the foolish who go into the cemetery to see the lights, and a bright light hits you in the face, on the other end of the light will probably be a big policeman holding a flashlight! The only thing you can say is, "boy, I am in a heap of trouble!"

Gamma Rays

After I was promoted to Detective Sergeant in plainclothes, I tried to fit in with the Detective Department, but for some reason always felt out of place. Cases the other men didn't want were held over until I came in and then given to me. I was given some lulu assignments, but I took them on and did the best I could.

This particular case was one of the hold-overs. I'll always remember this one. When I walked into the squad room and saw that everyone was grinning sheepishly, I knew it was a good one. I picked up the paperwork from my basket and went up to the front where the daily reports were kept.

Just outside the door, I stopped. I heard one of the guys say, "Wait until he sees what he got this time!"

I knew then I had been given an assignment that no one else wanted. I picked up the daily reports and went to the conference room to read them. After I read the daily reports, I looked at what had been in my work basket. It was a report stating someone was harassing a lady who lived on Long Chaney Street. It seemed at night someone was shining lights in her windows. The report stated that a patrol car had answered several calls there. The patrol officers requested that a detective talk to this lady. I noticed that the request had not been followed up on. The front office had picked it up and sent it to the detectives. I didn't understand why the report had been held and given to me unless it was one of the calls no one wanted. I was soon to learn.

I was working the 5 p.m. until 1 a.m. shift. Soon the room emptied out as the other detectives went home. I worked on some paperwork for a while, then decided I had better go and talk to the lady on Long Chaney Street. Long Chaney Street is across from the Georgia Power maintenance buildings. At the time of this incident there was an open field that led down to the river. A dirt road ran from the Turner McCall side of the railroad under the trestle and back out onto Long Chaney. It was a well-known lover's lane for young people at that time. There were always cars going in and out of there at night. It was a well-patrolled area. I remember thinking this would be simple to explain to the lady.

It was getting dark when I pulled up in front of the house. I was met by a small woman who must have been in her eighties. After I introduced myself, she motioned for me to come inside quickly. I did.

She said, "Sit in that chair and you'll be safe. The rays don't hit that chair."

The rays don't hit that chair? When she said that, it threw me for I had no idea what she was talking about.

"The rays?" I asked.

"Yes. Didn't they tell you?"

"No. The just wanted me to come and talk to you about your problem."

The lady started to tell me about aliens from outer space who landed in the field across from her house. She said they would get out there at night and shoot her house with gamma rays. I listened, not believing what I was hearing. It was obvious she was frightened of the gamma rays. Then she said something I couldn't believe. She said that a police officer had told her just stay inside and she would be all right.

I asked her if another police officer had been out to talk to her and she replied there had been two out there that morning. They told her they would send someone back out that evening who could take care of her problem.

My expression must have changed because she asked, "Is everything all right?"

"Yes, everything is all right." The two officers who had come out that morning had to have been two other detectives. I asked her if she had someone who I could talk to about her problem.

"My son lives a few doors down the street."

I got the house number and told her I would come back after I talked to her son.

I got in the car and backed down the street to where her son lived. He was standing on the porch waiting for me when I got out of the car. I told him who I was and we began to discuss the problem that his mother had. We both knew that what she was seeing was car headlights. After a while I came to the conclusion that her windows needed to be sealed so that light couldn't get into the house at night.

He said he had put up dark shades, but that had not helped. I told him about a similar case where aluminum foil was put over the windows to keep the light out. He got in the car with me and we went back to discuss it with the lady to see if she would agree for him to put the foil on her windows. She agreed for him to do it the next day, so I left with the understanding that he would let me know if it worked.

It was several weeks before I heard from him. He told me that the foil kept the lights out and she was happy that none of the gamma ray could get though to her. I made out a report and turned it in to the supervisor that night before I left for home. I felt good that the problem had been solved for her. The one thing I never understood was, who could tell an old lady that aliens from another planet were bombarding her house with gamma rays? I believed then, as I still do today, that it was a very cruel thing to scare an old lady like that.

Light in the Window

All police have had calls that will stay in their memory. This is one of mine. It happened in the late 70s or early 80s. A call went out to one of my police cars to see a fellow on East Fourth Street about lights in a house that was being remodeled. I was close by, so I told dispatch that I would back up the unit on the call. I arrived on the scene before the car that was actually dispatched and met the neighbor who had called. He stated that the house was being remodeled and no one was supposed to be in it. We went over to the house and began a search of the doors and windows to see if any were opened. But all were locked. With no way to get in we went back over to the neighbor's house. We assured him that all doors and window were locked tight and we couldn't find a way to get inside. I told him if he saw the lights again to give us a call and we'd be back.

The next night dispatch gave me a call back to the address on East Fourth Street. When I arrived, the same neighbor was standing out in front of his house. I checked out and went over to talk to him.

"Up there," he pointed, "in that window! I just saw it a few minutes ago."

"What was there?" I asked.

"The light in the window," he replied. "I stood out here and watched it before I called you."

I started over to the house. He followed me still talking about what the light looked like.

"It glows," he said, "first bright then lighter and then it

disappeared."

I checked the doors and windows again to make sure someone had not broken in. Everything was locked up tight. No one could have gotten in without a key. We walked back to my patrol car and talked. I suggested he ask the man who was doing the remolding for a key or his phone number so we could call him. As I checked back in to service, I knew that I would be called out there again.

The next night was a busy one. It was getting late before we could take a break. Just as I had checked out to get something to eat, they gave me the call. I changed to a 'to go' order and ate en route to the address on East Fourth Street. I also asked dispatch to send me a backup unit. When I arrived the old fellow was waiting outside his house. We checked out and, getting the key from him, went inside. He stood outside and waited for us.

There were lumber and saws inside on the first floor. We began a search, looking in every closet and anywhere else someone might hide. Nothing on the first floor. We went upstairs and began a search of the second floor. Again, nothing.

I walked over to where the old gentleman said he had seen a light in the window. I stood there for a few minutes feeling the hairs on the back of my neck stand up. The space where I was standing seemed to be cold for some reason. I called my backup over to me.

"Can you feel the difference in the temperature over here?" I asked.

"It's colder over here than any other place in the house."

We went back outside where we assured the old fellow that there was no one in the house. I walked back over to the car and sat down in it.

I sat there a few minutes watching the old gentleman talking to the officer. He turned and came over to where I sat.

"Officer," he said, "I bet you think I am an old man who's lost his mind."

I assured him that I didn't think that. The other car checked back into service and left. I motioned for the old gentleman to come around and sit in the car. We sat there and talked for a while until I was about to leave, when suddenly the old fellow exclaimed, "Up there in the window!"

Did I get a shock when I saw what he was pointing at! There in the window was a light that seemed to let off a glow. It would glow real bright and then fade away. I quickly got out of the car and moved toward the house. I could see the window but there was nothing in it. I crept to the side of the house and there in the window directly over my head was the light. I was close this time and watched in amazement. Then as I stood and watched, it faded out and disappeared. I could not believe what I had seen and turned to go back to the patrol car. The old gentleman was pointing to the front window where the light was now seen. I stood on the ground and watched it in the window above. It would glow and then it would fade almost completely away. Then it disappeared again and I turned and went back to the patrol car.

I asked the old guy if he could explain it, but he shook his head. We agreed that there was no reason that a patrol car should be sent back up there on a call. The old gentleman went back into his house and I checked back in to service.

What did I see in the window of that house? I can't say. I will say that I saw a glowing light. But what it was, I don't know. When you read about some of the things that I've seen, you might say, "He believes in the supernatural." Or you might say, "that old man is plain nuts."

I know that I've seen things that I can't explain, whether 'plain nuts' or the supernatural.

Miracle

Back in the 70s, when I came out of plainclothes and went back into uniform as a sergeant, I had a situation happen that I haven't ever been able to explain. One day I was in the station fixing to go out on patrol when one of the dispatchers asked me to check on a car at the Duck Pond on Vaughn Road. I said sure and left the station. There had been a misty rain most of the day, but it had let up just at dark. I arrived at the Duck Pond to find a car on its side hanging precariously over the edge of the road. I immediately began a search of the car and the surrounding area. I looked the car over inside but no one was in it. I called dispatch for a wrecker and checked to see if anyone had gone to Floyd Medical Center. I searched down the bank but turned up no one, so began to gather information for a report while waiting for the wrecker.

I saw the wrecker as it turned from Turner McCall and recognized the driver as a friend of mine called Shorty. Shorty, for some reason, had always called me Mister Lonie.

He got out of the wrecker after greeting me and said, "This looked like a good one."

We walked around the car and Shorty determined the best way to pull the car upright. Shorty headed off to get the wrecker into position when a moan came from the car. We both stopped and looked at each other.

"Did you hear that?" I asked him.

He nodded and pointed toward the car. "Yes, it came from the car."

We both began to search for the source of the moan when we

heard it again. I got down on my knees and shined my flashlight underneath the overturned car. There in a space under the car I could see the body of a woman. I called for an ambulance.

"Shorty," I asked, "how are you going to get that car off the woman without crushing her?"

"I don't know," he said. "It has to be pulled from below so that it will go down the embankment. I can't get below it for the ground is muddy and the wrecker might get stuck."

Another moan came from under the car and a chill went up my back.

"The car has got to be moved so we can get the woman out!" I was standing by the car when the woman let out a scream that I will never forget. It was a scream of pure terror, like nothing I had ever heard before. How I was able to do what I did next I'll never know. I reached down, grabbed the car and lifted. The car seemed to shake and then it tumbled down the bank and landed upright on it wheels!

The ambulance pulled in right then and the woman was transferred to Floyd Medical Center. I sat down in my car and watched as Shorty pulled the car back up the bank and onto the road. He motioned for me to come over and pointed to a purse on the floor. He took the car key off a string of keys and gave the rest to me.

"It's yours," I said, motioning to the car. I started back to the patrol car but Shorty stopped me.

"Mister Lonie, what did you say just as you lifted the car off that woman?"

"Did I say something?"

You said something that I didn't catch and then the car fell over the embankment," he replied.

I remember shaking my head as I got into my patrol car and headed for the hospital. I didn't know what had happened; I only know that somehow the car moved over the embankment without crushing the woman underneath it.

I arrived at the hospital to find a miracle. The woman who had been trapped underneath the car was sitting up in a chair in the emergency center. She had a bandage on her forehead and some

POLICE WORK

scratches on her arms. I gave her the purse and took the information necessary for my report. I was amazed at how lucky she was. She had flipped a car, was thrown out, and escaped with only minor bruises.

I had worked many wrecks before this one and worked many more afterwards, but never worked another one like this again. When I got home after my shift, I felt like everything had been drained from me.

The next day I was still trying to figure out how that car had tumbled down the embankment when I lifted up on it. I went back to where the accident had happened and looked around. The space underneath the car where she had been trapped was so small! I couldn't understand how she hadn't been crushed. Somehow the edge of the road had kept the car off her. The thing that was bothering me was how did I get strong enough to lift the car and send it over the embankment? I know that I am not strong enough to turn over a car. The only explanation that I could come up with was that the wheels of the car were hanging over the embankment, so when I attempted to move the car, it didn't have far to go before it slid over. I remember getting back into the patrol car and looking back at the place where the wreck happened. I remember thinking that a miracle had happened.

I also wondered about what Shorty had asked me. "What did you say when you grabbed the side of the car and turned it back onto the wheels?" I cannot answer that question for I don't know. I don't remember too much about what happened when I grabbed hold of that car. There are some things in life that can never be explained.

Don't Forget Me, Mister

I've heard of people who could forget bad memories by removing them from their mind. I've chosen to keep all my memories, good or bad. Once I was promoted to the rank of Detective Sergeant, I was placed in the plainclothes division on the five p.m. to one a.m. shift. This shift dealt with a lot of shoplifting cases.

Lonie Adcock as Detective

This particular incident involved a call to a grocery store to pick up a shoplifter. I remember it as if it happened yesterday. I responded to the call and when I arrived at the store, I was told they were holding the suspect in the manager's office. As I approached the office, I saw a little old lady standing in front of a rack of cakes. She appeared to be eating one of the cakes. As I approached the two men who were standing there with her, one of them walked off.

"You called the police?" I asked the one remaining.

He pointed to the little old lady. "Take her and charge her with shoplifting."

I looked at the little old lady and I knew he could see the disbelief on my face. She had to be at least eighty years old and couldn't have weighed more than seventy five pounds. I watched as she ate the cake she had taken from the rack.

Turning to the clerk, I asked, "Are you going to prosecute this old lady?"

"Yes," he replied. "The manager wants her put in jail for shoplifting."

"Look at her!" I said. "She's no thief! She's an old lady who's hungry."

"I know, but I have to do what the manager says!"

"Where is the manager?"

The clerk pointed toward a closed door. I headed that way.

The clerk called after me, "He doesn't want to talk to you!"

I know I replied, "Tough! He *will* talk to me."

I tried to open the door but it was locked. I knocked and a girl opened it.

"I want to talk to the store manager," I told her.

She opened the door and I walked in to the office. The manager sat behind his desk with a frown on his face. He made it quite plain he didn't want to talk to me. Taking a chair that was in front of his desk, I plopped it down next to him. He had to swivel to look at me.

"What can I do for you, detective?" he asked.

"We need to talk about that old lady you have out there."

"I want her prosecuted for shoplifting."

"I can't put her in jail for shoplifting," I replied.

He smirked and said, "And tell me why not?"

"She has done no shoplifting."

"She took a cake from the rack and ate it!" the manager exclaimed.

"That's theft, not shoplifting."

We sat there for a good thirty minutes arguing back and forth. I finally got him to agree to let me pay for the cake with a promise that she wouldn't come back in his store. I put the little old lady in the car with the understanding there would be no prosecuting for her eating the cake.

On the way to the station, I stopped and picked up a hamburger and some fries. When we arrived, I took her to our break room, bought her a coke and sat her down to eat. A female dispatcher was on duty and I explained to her what was going on. I asked her to meet with the old lady and try to find out her name and where she lived. Meanwhile, I called family services and explained the situation. The lady from family services said she was not familiar with her, but she would call some of the case workers to try to find someone who was.

Then I went back to the break room to see if the dispatcher had found out anything. She explained that the old lady didn't know what her name was or where she lived. The other dispatcher came to the door and said I had a call from family services. I picked up the telephone and the lady explained to me that she was familiar with the case and told me to meet her at a First Avenue address. Apparently that was where the old lady lived.

So I took the lady to the address on First Avenue. The caseworker was waiting for us. She explained that the old lady lived by herself, but recently she had begun to develop dementia. The only known relative, a son, lived somewhere in Tennessee. She said she had a telephone number and would get in touch with him tomorrow. She wanted me to go in the house with her and look around. The door was unlocked and the lights were on, so we went inside. I noticed that the mailbox was stuffed full of mail, so I took the stack and placed it on a table in the living room. Everything looked to be all right so I showed the lady the stack of mail. There were several checks in the stack. There was no food in the house. I often wondered how long that old lady had gone without food before eating the cake at the store.

The case worker explained she would take the lady to a safe place where she would receive care until her son could be notified. We found a key for the house, locked up, and went out to the street where the lady was waiting. I tried to escort her to the caseworker's car, but she pulled back and headed over to my car. I explained to her that she would have to go with the lady. Up till now, she hadn't spoken a word to me, but now she mumbled something that I didn't catch, but have wondered about all these years.

The next day when I arrived at work, I had a message to call the lady from family services, who told me the son had come down and taken her back to Tennessee. It was good to hear that the little old lady had been taken care of. I hoped that I would never run across a case like this ever again.

Those words she mumbled to me sure did sound like, "Don't forget me, mister."

Ghost Doll

I had been on the police force for a few years when I put in for the detective department. I was told that I couldn't get it, but I put in my name anyway. When the board interviewed the applicants, they laughed and told me to forget it. Much to everyone's surprise, a few days later a letter was posted stating that I had been promoted to the rank of Detective Sergeant. The plainclothes division had their own set of rules, but I thought I could eventually fit in. I knew that I had a rough road to travel but got ready for it.

I was placed on the five p.m. to one a.m. shift. I was ignored at first. Then I began to get the calls no one else wanted. I was called into the supervisor's office one day, given an address and told to see if I could stop the lady at the address from calling the supervisor. I took the address back to my desk. I noticed the other fellows grinning. I watched as they looked at each other and then back at me.

I stood up and announced, "Okay fellows, tell me what the joke is and I'll join in the fun."

No one said anything so I left the room and went up front to read the daily reports. I took the piece of paper from my pocket and read the name and North McLin address as well as these words: see this person at 11:15 tonight. I wondered why so late at night? The supervisor came down the hallway, so I asked him.

"She works late," he said and kept walking.

After reading the reports I went back to my desk and took out a forgery case that I had been working on.

The other fellows began to talk and, while pretending to work on a report, I listened. I picked up my paperwork, placed it in a folder, got my car keys, and left the room. I had just stepped into the hall when the men in the room let out a loud roar of laughter. I stepped back in and they got quiet. You could have heard a pin drop, it was so quiet. I didn't say anything, just turned and left the room. I got in my car and left the station. It took a few hours for my temper to cool down, but I finally went back to the station. All the others had gone home. The Detective Department was empty except for me. It was getting late. I worked on the forgery report for a while and decided to go eat. I left the station after telling the dispatcher that I would be out on a call later that night.

The time to meet the lady on North McLin arrived and I headed that way. I pulled in front of the house, checked out and a woman on the porch got up and met me.

"You the man from the police department?" she asked.

I showed her my identification and she let me in. Not knowing what this was about, I followed her inside. She began to turn on lights and soon the house was as bright as sunlight.

"Now," she said, "if you don't give me a smirk like that man who was here this morning, I will show you what I got."

I followed her to a back bedroom where she turned on the light.

"There," she pointed, "see that doll lying on the floor?"

I nodded my head and said I did.

"That doll was on that shelf when I left here this morning." She pointed to a type of chest that had shelves in it. "I left that doll on that shelf," she said going over and putting her hand on one of the shelves.

"Hold on a minute," I said. "Are you telling me someone is putting that doll in the floor while you're at work?"

"Yes. It happens every day since I brought that doll home with me."

"Have you checked your doors and windows to see if someone has broken into your house?"

"I have and no one has broken in," she replied.

I picked up the doll from the floor and a cold chill went up my back. I noticed she was watching me in an odd way. I put the doll

225

on a table and turned. The lady was staring at me.

"Is something the matter?" I asked.

"Did you feel something cold just now?"

I whirled and looked out in the hall. I thought I had seen movement out of the corner of my eye. I walked out into the hall and got the surprise of my life. There appeared to be a small girl peeping around the door from a room at the end of the hall!

I smiled and turned back to the woman who was standing in the middle of the room with a funny look on her face.

"You have a small girl?" I asked her.

She shook her head no.

"There in the room at the end of the hall I saw a small girl," I said. I reached in my pocket for my small flashlight and started down the hall to the room. She followed close behind me. I shined the light in the room and saw nothing.

"Officer, on the right side of the door is a light switch."

I reached around, turned on the light, and began a search of the room but found no one. I looked everywhere a small child might hide but found nothing. I even pulled out the drawers in a dresser making sure that she had not gotten into one of them. There was no one in that room but I *know* that I saw a small child peeping around the door. I went back to the room where the doll was and picked it up. Again a cold chill went up my back. I placed the doll on the very top shelf, pushing it back to where a child could not reach it.

As I left, I told the woman I would come back the following night to see if the doll was still on the shelf. I went in to headquarters and signed out for the night, thinking about what I had seen peeping at me from the door. The next evening when I went in to work, the fellows sat around grinning. I didn't say anything, just signed in and started to work up a case on the forgery that I had been working on. The smiles and the snickering in the hallway went on. I chose to ignore it for the time being.

Our supervisor came in and said to me, "You must have done something right because I didn't get a call from that woman on North McLin."

I looked up and smiled. He went into his office and got ready to go home. I went on to finish the forgery case and almost forgot to go back to North McLin. The dispatcher informed me that I had a call from her. I told him I was en route and to tell her to stand by.

As I pulled into her driveway, I saw she was waiting on the porch with another woman.

"Thought you had forgot me," she said.

"I got busy and had to be reminded," I told her. "Have you been inside the room?"

"No," she said. "I've been waiting on the front porch with my friend until you got here."

We headed for the room with the doll in it. When the lights came on we saw the doll lying in the middle of the floor! I looked at the woman and knew that there was no way that she could have gotten the doll off the shelf without a ladder. I picked up the doll and got that chill up my back again. I put the doll on the table and went to look at the door of the other bedroom. I wasn't surprised to see what looked like a small face peeping around it. The two women were staring at me.

"Would you like my opinion about what I would do if I lived here and this was happening to me?" I asked them.

She nodded.

I said, "I would get rid of that doll, find me another place and move."

The women followed me out to the front porch and I waited to see what the one with the doll had to say.

"Officer, I appreciate what you've done and I will take your advice!"

I left feeling as if I'd been in a cooler for a while.

A few weeks later I got a telephone call from he. She stated that she'd sold the doll to a furniture store. She had rented an apartment off Kingston Avenue. She told me that she had had no more problems since she had moved.

I often wondered if I saw what I thought I saw that night in the house on North McLin. Odd things sometimes happen that some call paranormal happenings. Some call them ghosts. Being skeptical I just say there are some things you can't explain and some things are better left alone.

The snickering at work stopped and my supervisor got no more calls from the woman who lived on North McLin. And I was glad I never had to go back in that house on North McLin!

Part 5

This & That

1911

The year was 1911 when Henry Ford built the car of all cars. Fuel for this car was sold only in drug stores. These cars were shipped to assembly plants all over Americ and several foreign countries in knocked down form. They cars were built at the Highland Park plant in Detroit, Michigan. Factory color was dark blue and all models were supplied with tops, windshields, and head lamps as standard equipment. Ford believed that nothing else was needed on his cars and the warranties would be void if anything else was added. Approximately 40,000 of these cars were built.

That car was the mighty Model T Ford. The commercial Runabout in 1911 sold for $680 FOB Detroit. According to information I found, there were only 8,000 cars and 144 miles of paved roads in 1911. The maximum speed limit was 10 miles per hour.

In 1911 only 14 percent of homes had bathtubs. There are still people out there who remember taking a bath in a galvanized wash tub. Throughout the week you washed with a rag from a small pan. I have always believed that the old saying "I took a bath on Saturday night whether I needed it or not" came from those days. On Saturday the old wash tub was filled and the kids would get in line for their weekly bath. The girls always got to go first at our house. You can imagine what the water looked like after the last boy in a large family finished bathing!

Only 8 percent of households had telephones. Can you imagine going to town and not seeing anyone with a telephone sticking out their ears? The reason you didn't see new cars and houses didn't have telephones was simple. The average wage paid was 22 cents an hour. The average U.S worker made $200 to $400 per year. A competent accountant could make up to $2,000 per year. A dentist could make up to $2,500 a year. A veterinarian could earn between $1,500 and $4,000 per year. A mechanical engineer could earn up to $5,000 per year. That put the $680.00 Model T out of reach of most people.

Ninety percent of all doctors had no college education. They attended so-called medical schools, many of which were condemned in the press. They read medical books written by more educated doctors. There were those folks in the community who could set a broken bone or treat a bruise or cut. They weren't doctors but were more like the midwife. More than 65 percent of births took place in the home. Most records of birth and deaths were kept by someone in the family. In 1911 the leading causes of death were pneumonia, influenza, tuberculosis, diarrhea, heart disease and stroke.

Groceries were considered expensive back then. Sugar cost four cents a pound and eggs were fourteen cents a dozen. Coffee had risen to fifteen cents a pound. Women only washed their hair once a month and used Borax or egg yolk for shampoo.

Canada passed a law prohibiting poor people from entering their country for any reason. The American Flag had only 45 stars. Two out of every adult couldn't read or write and only 6 percent of Americans had graduated from high school. Marijuana, heroin and morphine were available over the counter at the corner drugstore. There were about 230 murders reported in the entire U.S.A. The population of Las Vegas, Nevada was only 30.

Looking back over the past 100 years makes you wonder what is in store for us over the next hundred years.

Franklin Automobile

Several times I've written about the big black automobile that my half-brother John drove. I was in awe of that car as a small boy, and so I thought I would do some research on it. I remember that it was a Franklin. Many people nowadays have never heard of Franklins. That car was long and sleek and had room in it you wouldn't believe! I don't know what year or model John had, for I was a small boy at that time and it didn't matter anyway when I was sitting in it beside John. Riding in that car was like being in heaven, riding down the road and having people stare as you passed by!

Franklin automobile company can claim the distinction of building America's first successful gasoline powered motor car incorporating an air-cooled engine. Herbert H. Franklin and engineer John Wilkinson leveraged Wilkinson's participation in bicycle racing into designing a gas powered horseless carriage. During the summer of 1898, Wilkinson had developed a single cylinder air cooled gasoline engine. He demonstrated his first automobile on January 1, 1900. In November 1901 Franklin manufacturing company was restructured to produce the Franklin Automobile.

Wilkinson put his bicycle racing experience to use in fielding Franklin Auto in races and endurance events. A Franklin set a record in the 1904 transcontinental run. The Franklin had the distinction of having the first four cylinder engine introduced in 1902. Most cars at that time had a single or two cylinder engine. By the middle of the decade, the company offered an updated single product line with prices ranging from $2,300 to $3,400. Franklin noted that closed car sales exceeded those of open cars. Eighty percent of Franklin's 1923 production was closed cars.

By 1927 the wooden frame had been replaced by a steel frame. It was possible to buy 27 different series of Franklins. The Franklin was the first American car with aluminum pistons. Cooling was aided after 1910 by the adaptation of a squirrel cage fan incorporated in the rear mounted flywheel. This sucked air though the sealed bonnet over the cylinders. The 1912 model had a newly redesigned bonnet plus full pressure lubrication. 1922 the Franklin range was restyled, acquiring a rounded dummy radiator inside of which was a fan. The fan forced air up to the top of the bonnet down over the cylinder fins and crankcase and out beneath the car. This pattern of radiator did not last long. By 1925 the Franklin was breaking new ground with the J. Frank De Causes style Series 11 with a handsome square cut radiator with vertical chrome strips across the grille. Franklin's last model was the Olympic, but this was a Franklin in engine only. All the rest was cheap. It was as unsuccessful as its more expensive stablemate and in 1934 the factory produced it last car.

U.S.A.

My days at Elm Street School all began the same way: walking to school and beginning our day with a prayer and the Pledge of Allegiance to the flag. Prayer was as much a part of the learning system as all the other subjects we had. Now they say that prayer in school has offended some people and must go. Did they ask the majority of the people if they were offended or did they take the word of a few? In the land where the majority rules, what happened?

I remember the big flag that sat in the classroom at Elm Street School. I remember the Pledge of Allegiance said "under God, with liberty and justice for all." I remember when the Japanese attacked Pearl Harbor and how the nation stood still, waiting to see how many lives had been lost. The call went out and every red blooded American answered the call. People who had never had a weapon in their hands were willing and ready to defend this great country. Defend it they did—from island to island to the island of Japan they fought. The flag went up and flew proudly. Those who saw it knew it was the flag of a proud and great nation. Good men died defending it and now a small group of people want it removed from the classroom because it offends them. I wonder if those people had a mother, father, sister, brother or any other relative die defending that great flag? Remove our flag from our property? No way, if my flag offends you, then leave my property and go back where you came from. If the flag representing the country that you came from does not offend you, then go back to that country and stay.

This country was founded on freedom of religion and the right to worship as you choose. Here of late, a small group of people have brought lawsuit after lawsuit against religion. When I was growing up, businesses had religious themes hanging on the wall. It was not uncommon to see a picture of one of the founders of this country on one wall and the Ten Commandment on another. A picture of Christ and the Last Supper might hang on the foyer wall. I can't recall the business that had a picture of Moses on the mountain hanging in the foyer, but I always thought that it was one of the most beautiful paintings I had ever seen.

I was listening to a news segment the other morning about some people in bleachers yelling, "U.S.A!" to show pride in their country's team. Now of all things, some people were offended. They don't want them hollering "U.S.A." any more. I couldn't believe this would offend someone at a game or a rally or anywhere else. This is your country! Take pride and yell "God bless the U.S.A." loud enough for all the other countries to hear you. If they don't like it, let them stay away from the good old U.S.A.

Everywhere you go, you hear about someone being offended by one thing or another. I was at a department store a few days ago when I heard a shuffling noise. Turning around, I saw a big fat man who was wearing a pair of what I call "butt pants." The straddle of the pants was down to his knees and his shorts were showing, exposing the small crack above them. He had a telephone stuck in his ear and was using foul language. He was talking loudly enough so everyone could hear him. A lady with two small children was walking along an aisle. The guy turned and almost ran over the children. He never let up on his foul language even in front of the woman and her kids. Did this offend the people who had to listen to his foul mouth? I don't know about anyone else, but it sure did me.

I listened to a news report about a swastika being painted on a church. The news reporter talked to the Reverend and some of his Deacons. My heart went out to these people. Anyone who would do something like that needs to be deported to some other country. If that country knew about the swastika, they probably wouldn't let the person in. These types of people need to be put somewhere with their kind on a deserted island.

These are some of my opinions. You have the right to disagree with them. I have always heard that opinions are something that everyone has. Like everything else, some opinions stink. Who knows? Mine may be some of those that stink, but they are mine and I'll stick with them. I will defend prayer whether it is in school, church, home or public. Old Glory I will defend, as the song says, "until then." If I am at a rally or anywhere else and I decide to stand up and shout "U.S.A.! U.S.A.!" I will do so. If you're offended by what I've said, get your head out of the sand and look around. What you see happening might just wake you up. This is your country. Don't let it be taken away from you—Americans.

Born on the Fourth of July

The year 1776 saw the birth of a nation. On June 11, the colonies' second Continental Congress, which met in Philadelphia, formed a committee. A document was drafted by Benjamin Franklin, John Adams, Roger Sherman and Robert R. Livingston to break all ties with England. The final version of the document that we know as the Declaration of Independence was officially adopted by the Continental Congress on July 4th. On July 5th copies of the document was distributed and on July 6, the *Pennsylvania Evening Post* was the first to print it. On July 8, 1776 the Declaration of Independence was read publicly in Philadelphia Square to the ringing of bells and band music. One year later on July 4, 1777 Philadelphia marked Independence Day by adjourning Congress and celebrating with bonfires and fireworks.

Other towns throughout the colonies began to take up the practice of celebrating the 4th of July. The holiday grew throughout the years and is now celebrated all over the United States of America. July the 4th was declared a federal holiday by Congress in 1941.

In July of 1776, 2.5 million people were estimated to be living in the United States. The liberty bell was cast twice, but due to defects, it had to be melted down and cast a third time. The first July 4th party held at the White House was in 1801. The stars on the original flag were cast in a circle to symbolize that all the colonies were equal. The 4th of July fact surrounding the term Uncle Sam was finally clarified and popularized during the war of 1812. Congress did not adopt Uncle Sam as a national symbol until 1961. Uncle Sam became synonymous with servitude as in "Uncle Sam Wants You."

The 4th of July is celebrated in different ways. Families celebrate by having friends and family over for cookouts. There are parades in most cities with a military escort to make it official.

Last but not least on July the 4th, 1930 Lonie B. Adcock made his first appearance, born to farmer Landum Benjamin Adcock and his wife Margaret Melissia Haney Adcock in Bartow County, Georgia. He was born American by heritage and Southern by the grace of God, a true southern American born on the 4th of July.

Star Spangled Banner

Christian Francis Scott Key was born August 1, 1779 in Carroll County, Maryland. He died January 11, 1883 at age 63 in Baltimore, Maryland. He was an American lawyer, author and an amateur poet. He wrote the lyrics to one of the most popular songs in the United States of America—"The Star Spangled Banner," our National Anthem.

During the war of 1812, Key, accompanied by the American Prisoner Exchange Agent John Skinner dined aboard the British ship HMS *Tonnant* as the guest of three British officers. Skinner and Key were there to negotiate the release of prisoners, one being Dr. William Beanes. Beanes was a resident of Marlboro, Maryland. He had been captured by the British after he had placed some rowdy stragglers under citizen's arrest. Key, Skinner and Beanes were not allowed to return to their ship because they had become familiar with the strength and position of the British units. The British intended to attack Baltimore. As a result of the detainment, Key had to watch the bombarding of the American forces at Fort Henry. When the smoke cleared, Key was able to see an American flag still waving.

On his way back to Baltimore, Key wrote a poem describing what he had seen. The poem was published in *The Patriot* on September 20, 1814. Key had intended to fit the poem to the rhythm of John Stafford Smith's "To Anacreon in Heaven." This was a popular tune Key had already used as a setting for his 1805 song "When the Warriors Return." The earlier song is also Key's original use of the phrase "star spangled flag." The fourth stanza urged the adoption of "In God is our Trust" as the national motto. Under the name "The Star Spangled Banner," the song was adopted as the American national anthem by an executive order from President Woodrow Wilson in 1916. This had little effect beyond requiring military bands to play it. A congressional resolution signed by President Herbert Hoover made it official.

Most of us have grown up going to ball games and other public gatherings where the National Anthem is played before they start. I can recall hearing this song being sung beautifully and also hearing it sung terribly! There are some who can sing it and some who cannot. Kate Smith was one who could sing it beautifully. Those who can't sing our anthem should leave it alone!

I saw in the paper where someone asked if it might be time for a new national anthem. Will those people go to Washington and get it changed? Will the majority of the people get to have a say? Will you wake up one morning and read in the paper and hear on television that there is now a new national anthem? Will it be like a lot of other things we have gotten from Washington: here it is— take it and like it? If it comes down to where people want a change, shouldn't it be put on a ballot? Shouldn't everyone get to vote on what the new anthem would be?

Wake up, people, before you get something else taken from you that you want to keep and something shoved down your throats that will choke you.

(Francis Scot Key facts courtesy of Wikipedia)

Flag Draped Coffin

Have you ever watched a military funeral and wondered about the flag draped coffin? Did you wonder why the flag was draped over the coffin and why it is folded with such precision when taken from the coffin? All Americans should know why the flag is draped as it is and why it is folded as it is.

Our founding fathers used God's words and teachings to establish our great nation. It is time that Americans get re-educated about this country's history and be proud of this country. Be proud of those who serve to protect our God-given rights and freedoms.

The 21 gun salute at military funerals represents the sum of the numbers in 1776. And the Honor Guard pays meticulous attention to correctly folding the United States of America's flag thirteen times. Most people think the 13 folds symbolize the original 13 colonies, but here is the real meaning.

The 1st fold is a symbol of life.

The 2nd fold is a symbol of the belief in eternal life.

The 3rd fold is made in honor and remembrance of the veteran departing the ranks who gave a portion of his life for the defense of the country in the attempt to attain peace throughout the world.

The 4th fold represents man's weaker nature. As American citizens trusting in God, it is to Him we turn in times of peace as well as in times of war for His divine guidance.

The 5th fold is a tribute to our country. In the words of Stephen Decatur, "Our country, in dealing with other countries, may she always be right, but she is still our country, right or wrong."

The 6th fold is where the heart lies. It is with their heart that soldiers pledge allegiance to the flag of the United States of America, and to the Republic for which it stands, one nation under God, indivisible, with Liberty and Justice for all.

The 7th fold is a tribute to the Armed Forces, for it is the Armed Forces that protect this country and our flag against all her enemies.

The 8th fold is a tribute to the one who entered into the valley of death that we might see the light of day.

The 9th fold is a tribute to womanhood and mothers for it has been though their faith, love, loyalty and devotion that the character of the men and women who have made this country great has been molded.

The 10th fold a tribute to fathers, for they too have given sons and daughters for the defense of their country.

The 11th fold represents the lower portion of the seal of King David and King Solomon and glorifies in the Hebrew eyes the God of Abraham, Isaac and Jacob.

The 12th fold represents eternity and glorifies in Christian eyes God the Father, the Son and the Holy Spirit.

The 13th fold places the stars uppermost reminding us of our nation's motto "In God We Trust."

After the flag is completely folded, it takes on the appearance of a cocked hat. The cocked hat reminds us of those who served under General George Washington, and the sailors and Marines who served under Captain John Paul Jones, who were followed by their comrades and shipmates in the Armed Forces of the United States, preserving for them the rights, privileges and freedoms we enjoy today.

Share this with the ones you love and all others. In the future when you see flags folded, you will know why. In the meantime, may God protect us always and may we remain one nation under God, with Liberty and Justice for all.

Looking Back

My family moved from the country to town when farming had about played out. My father worked construction until he passed away when I was eleven years old. This left my mother with three small boys and a girl to take care of. She was a seamstress who found work in a sewing room. In a few years my sister got married leaving my mother with just my two brothers and me. We were doing okay for a while until my mother got down with back problems. There was no one to help out so it fell on me—the oldest boy. I was fourteen at the time.

There was no choice left but quit school and go to work. For the last school year, I had been working in a cafe and going to school when I could. At the end of the school year my teacher told me that even though I had passed all my tests, I would have to go to summer school to make up lost time before she could pass me to the next grade. There were many days I had to work at the café until two o'clock in the morning, so I would not go to school the next day.

When my teacher told me about the summer school, I told her that there was no way I could do that. My family needed me to work to bring in money. I left school that day with a heavy heart for I knew that I would not go back to school again. Unlike most of the boys I went to school with, I liked school.

When I got home, I told my mother what had happened. Like me, she had no answer for me making up time at summer school. I went outside to the swing I had made for my younger brothers to play on and sat down. I put my head in my hands and did what a boy with a broken heart does: I had myself a good cry. Then I dried my tears and went to work at the cafe.

I had started out washing dishes but when the lady got behind in her orders, I would jump in and help her. Buddy, the man who ran the café, had noticed me helping her and talked to the lady whose name was Rose. Rose told him without my help she couldn't keep up the orders as they came in. Buddy called Rose and me into his office one night after closing. I wondered what I had done for I was sure he was going to fire me. He smiled when he saw I was nervous.

"Rose," he said, "I've hired you a helper in the kitchen to help you cook."

Rose smiled and asked, "Is it anyone I know?"

I found out later that Rose knew what was going on.

Buddy answered, "Let me see." He picked up a paper from his desk. "The name of your new helper is Lonie."

That floored me! My mouth opened but no words came out.

Buddy then said, "And that's not all. He gets a raise on his paycheck!"

So my first full time job was a short order cook. I worked there most of the summer until I was found out. Someone had told Buddy I was too young to work there. He had to let me go. It broke my heart because I had gotten used to working with Rose, whom I have never forgotten. Out of a job, I started to look for something that a young boy could do.

I took on anything I could find. I worked for P.D. Shahan at a seed and feed store on West Third. I was told when I was hired that it would be a temporary job. It lasted though the winter. Come spring I was back out hunting and found a job working for Hugh Johnson Construction fixing up fences and such on a race track that was behind the levee where the ball fields are now. I cut grass with a cousin of mine during that summer. Someone told me that a plumbing company who was doing construction work on the new school at Coosa needed some ditch diggers. I got the job and fell in digging ditches for the septic lines. That job lasted into the next year and then I was back to looking again. A friend of mine told me about a company on East First Street by the name J.P. Roberts Construction Company. I asked for and got a job there. I was sixteen at the time and for the next four years I worked for and with some good people. From there I joined the Army Signal Corps. Once out of the Army I was hired by the Rome Police Department and was there until I retired. I worked with many good people down though the years

When I lived in Fourth Ward on what was called the short end of West Ninth Street, things were good. That is where the Western Sizzlin' Cafe now sits. My friend Jimmy, who lived next door, moved to the very end of West 7th Street down against the levee where the street turned and came out on Fifth Avenue. West 7th no longer exists. Nowadays it is Turner McCall Boulevard. West 7th Street had two houses on it before it made a turn. It is Bale Street today.

I soon became friends with the fellow who lived next door to Jimmy. He read comic book and always had a stack of them. I would sit on his front porch and read them. He had two daughters who were five and seven years old. The five year old was a small, skinny girl and noisy! I would be reading and she would come up the steps making a racket. Once she went inside, I'd return to reading. Here she would come again making that noise. I remember saying to myself, *Girls! Do we really need them?*

Time went by and slowly I drifted away from old friends as we grew up. I hadn't seen the little girl for quite a few years, until I was in the Army. A friend and I had come home for a weekend. Another friend had come with us and we were driving around the block on Broad Street when I saw these two girls. I recognized one of them as the little noisy one. I got out of the car and walked down to the First Avenue Theater with her and her friend. She didn't seem so bad any more!

I didn't see her again until I was out of the Army. We had written to each other all during my Army stint. We were married about a year after I got out. Fifty eight years later, we are still married and with the grace of God will stay married for the rest of our lives.

I've worked most of my life but have no regrets. I made it a habit to read everything I could get while growing up. I have always tried to learn as much as possible. With the help of that good woman, I have accomplished the goals that I set.

But there was one thing that so many others had that I didn't. I remember that day when I sat in the swing with a broken heart because I had to quit school and go to work. I was so sure I could never have a High School Diploma. Later on, I studied hard and earned my G.E.D. from the school system. I see pictures of people with the cap and gown holding their diplomas and it gives me a funny feeling in the pit of my stomach. The one thing that I always wanted was a picture of me in a cap and gown holding a diploma with my name on it: Lonie Burton Adcock

Butts

At one point, my wife had been in the hospital a fairly long time, and I sat right there with her. When I needed a break, I went outside to the gazebo that faced the emergency room door. I watched as people came and went, one of whom was an old gentleman. He held a walking stick in his hands. He would place the stick out in front of him and then walk up to it. I was amazed at how fast he could move. He headed to the gazebo and sat down opposite me.

He reached into his shirt pocket and took out a package of cigarettes. He sat for a moment staring at them, then held them out to me. "Smoke?" he asked.

I shook my head. "No thanks. I don't smoke."

He then returned his gazed to the cigarettes, turning the pack over in his hands.

"Nasty habit," he remarked as he lit one.

I sat quietly as he puffed. I could see he had something else he wanted to say.

He soon continued. "I didn't smoke until I went into the Army. In there we called them butts. I had a good friend who I went though basic training with. We would sit around the PX and smoke butts and drink a beer after training was over.

"It wasn't long before we were shipped overseas. We must have landed on every island in the Pacific Ocean. We would fight our way across one and they would load us up and away we'd go to another. It was on one of those islands that I lost my friend.

"I returned home with an Honorable Discharge, got married

and raised a family. I smoked butts halfway around the world and now here in my own country, I've become a menace to society. I no longer can smoke in a public building which I helped to pay for. I gotta go outside no matter what the weather is like. It will only be a matter of time before they stop you from smoking in your own house."

He slowly stood up and turned to me. I watched his lips tremble as he spoke.

"I wonder if I will be permitted though the pearly gates with a pack of butts in my shirt pocket?"

I smiled as he left the gazebo and walked back toward the emergency room. The automatic doors swung open for him and I believed that the Pearly Gates would do the same, even with a pack of butts in his shirt pocket.

Do You Know?

While checking my email recently, I came across an interesting article. I've never been to the place mentioned in the article, so I really enjoyed learning some intriguing facts.

As you walk up the steps to the building which houses the U.S. Supreme Court, you can see near the top of the building a row of the world's law givers. Each one is facing toward a figure standing in the middle of the group. That figure is Moses holding the Ten Commandments.

How did that happen? Someone must have slipped up. No, no one made a mistake. The figure of Moses was put there to remind us of the Ten Commandments of God. Did you know that there are Bible verses etched in stone all over the federal buildings and monuments in D.C? Did you know every session of Congress begins with a prayer by a preacher whose is paid by the taxpayers? This has been so since 1777.

Did you know that 55 founders of the Constitution were members of the established orthodox churches in the colonies? Did you know that James Madison, our fourth President, made the following statement: "We have staked the whole of all our political institutions upon the capacity of mankind for self government; upon the capacity of each and all of us to govern ourselves, to control ourselves according to the Ten Commandments of God."

Something must have gone wrong for suddenly everything we have done for the past 220 years in this country is wrong. Did you know that this country was built on the Holy Bible and belief in God? Let's bring back "One Nation Under God."

A little Humor Is Good For The Soul

Things that life has taught me not to do:

- You don't hug a gorilla
- You don't kiss an Alligator
- You don't put on boxing gloves with a kangaroo
- You don't roller skate in a buffalo herd
- You don't stick out your tongue at a snake while looking him in the face
- You don't dance the rumba with an elephant
- You don't wrestle with a gorilla
- You don't run a foot race with a cheetah
- You don't go skinny dipping with a polar bear
- You don't wee wee off the pier. (If you do, watch out for the barracuda.)
- You don't walk backward while crossing the street
- You don't enter a butt-kicking contest if you have one leg
- You don't open your mouth while under a flock of pigeons
- You don't ever moon a werewolf

Obey the above and you will get through life without too many problems. If you have to choose only one, choose the last one. You must never, ever moon a werewolf. If you do, a heap of trouble awaits you! If you don't believe this, moon the first werewolf you see.

If you have enjoyed reading *Memories of an Old Geezer*, stand by for more Memories on their way. With his thinking cap on and his feeble mind in gear, the Old Geezer is back at the computer. Keep your eyes open! Who knows when the Old Geezer will appear!

Find the Old Geezer on the web at:
sites.google.com/site/loniebadcock

or email him: lbadcock@dishmail.net

CPSIA information can be obtained at www.ICGtesting.com
Printed in the USA
LVOW060343131211
259146LV00002B/1/P